A 30-DAY JOURNEY

OUT OF THE SHADOWS & INTO THE WORLD

Cover Design:
Brownie Designs, Birmingham, AL

Book Production:
Craftsman Printing, Inc., Birmingham, AL

TABLE OF CONTENTS:

Introduction:

Welcome to a journey of faith, friend. We are thrilled you have made a decision to make an impact on your world for Christ. This devotional was birthed in connection with a conference in Pigeon Forge, Tennessee titled, Emerge and Engage. It was basically a mandate for followers of Christ to emerge from the shadows and impact their communities. Joey Hill, Jonah Sorrentino (aka, KJ52), Scott Lenning, and I have prayed, studied, and applied what the Lord is teaching us to this devotional. We could not have done it without the help of Emily Osburne, who spent countless hours editing, Brownie Hill, who designed the book, and Kim Beverage, who served as the quarterback for the team.

This book is an outline for change. For several years, our conferences have revolved around finding your identity in Christ, discovering your spiritual gifts, and uncovering God's call for your life. However, a dear friend challenged us to give the students a mission to accomplish. He explained that he sees Christian students who are bored and ready for more. They want to see dramatic change in their lives and in their world.

Well, we know that most revolutions begin with the young, and young at heart. We expect this book to be challenging, but we know that, if you accept the challenge, you can begin a movement. If you get to the end of the thirtieth day and you have only READ, then our mission has failed.

Start now with the end in mind. How do you want to impact someone's life for eternity?

For over two thousand years, the Church has sought to emerge from the shadows to impact the world. How does this happen? From what do you need to emerge? You may need to emerge from pain, insecurity, or little sins that have grown to rule your life. It's time to surrender to the King and ask Him to use you as a vessel. The scope of your impact will be directly related to your surrender to Jesus.

After you surrender, you will focus on impact. The first fifteen days are intended to strip away anything that stands in your way. The next fifteen will be focused on engaging your world. This is not a devotional about a specific book of the Bible or a spiritual discipline.

It is a devotional to inspire action.

And not just any action.

Action that counts for eternity.

One of my favorite plays is the Broadway show, Les Miserables. It is a story of revolution. It is set in France, where a group of college students prepare for the day of change. Read their song and feel the pulse of their cry:

Do you hear the people sing?
Singing a song of angry men?
It is the music of a people
Who will not be slaves again!
When the beating of your heart
Echoes the beating of the drums
There is a life about to start
When tomorrow comes!

Will you join in our crusade?
Who will be strong and stand with me?
Beyond the barricade
Is there a world you long to see?

Then join in the fight
That will give you the right to be free!

We know that our country is on the verge of revolution. We will either see a spiritual revival or will begin to teach a nation to die with dignity. So, do you hear the beating drums? Let's make an impact together!

-Scott Dawson

PART I: EMERGE FROM

"You are my lamp, O Lord; the Lord turns my darkness into light."

- 2 Samuel 22:29

Everyone wants to make a difference.

In over twenty years of ministry, I've never met anyone who did not want his or her life to have an impact. No one intends to live an insignificant life.

If we all desire to make an impact, why are so few people successful in this endeavor? I believe it's due to an epidemic lack of vision. Most people are walking in darkness because they have not considered anything beyond today, beyond this month, and beyond the years of the life they will live on earth.

The truth is... in order to live in light of your purpose, you have got to consider the end of your life and work backwards. Have you ever wondered what people will say about you at your funeral? Have you ever considered what you would do if you only had a few months to live? Have you ever thought about heaven or about what God will say about you when you die?

Whoa.

That's serious.

It's so serious that many people avoid these questions completely. But I tell you friend, the answers to them are the keys to walking in light every day of your life.

A tombstone in England illustrates this idea. The epitaph reads, "Pause now stranger as you pass by; As you are alive so once was I; As I am dead, so you will be; Prepare for death and follow me." Under the epitaph, someone wrote the following words with a black Sharpie, "Follow you is not my intent, until I know which way you went!" This joke reveals tremendous truth. We all must pause and consider which way we will go. And only one man has conquered death, so let's follow him.

Let me explain.

We live in a world that is hopeless. Since we have all sinned, we are all separated from God, living in darkness, living without hope. Sin simply means we have fallen short of perfection. Even if you have told one lie, stolen a tiny pencil, or cheated on a single test, you are no longer perfect. Our unholy action reveals our choice to rebel against God.

God is loving, but He is also holy. Being holy, He cannot be in the presence of sin. We are separated from Him due to our sinfulness, not able to be with Him even on our BEST day.

Now, here is the good news! When we could not come to Him, He came to us. He sent His Son to pay a debt we owed. For thirty-three years He walked on this planet and not once did He say, "Pay Me" or "Thank Me" but He says, "Follow Me!" Why? Because He knew His mission.

He died. He was buried. On the third day He arose. No one has ever died, resurrected, and not died again except Jesus. Therefore, He is the only one who can issue life. He wants to give this life to you. It takes you receiving the gift. You can't buy it, negotiate it or bargain. You must surrender.

Salvation is not about believing the facts. Remember - The demons know Jesus is real. They understand that Jesus was resurrected. So, if you just believe, you have the same faith as a demon in hell. So, what is the difference? Romans 10:13 tells us, "Whosoever CALLS on the name of the Lord shall be saved." The term, call means, "To stretch out." If you were drowning, you would know you could not save yourself. You must grab the life preserver. Jesus saves you. However, you must receive Him into your life. It's up to you to reach out.

You must call upon Jesus and receive him in order to be saved.

So, have you received Christ into your life for the forgiveness of your sins? Are you ready for him to impact your life before you can effectively impact the world? I know no better way to receive Him than by a prayer.

The first step to emerging involves reaching out to Jesus. Grab the life preserver and emerge from darkness. Although repeating a prayer does not save you, calling out to Jesus does. On the next page is an example of the prayer of a person who is reaching toward God.

"Dear God. I know I have done some things wrong. But I know you love me to the point that you sent your Son to die on the cross. Right now, the best way I know how, I open up my heart and receive you into my life. Forgive me of my sins. Make me brand new. I know you love me. Help me to love you. Thank you God. I now call you Father."

If you just prayed this prayer, I would love to help you get started in your Christian walk. Let me know. My email is scott@scottdawson.org. You will also need to tell either your pastor or youth leader at church. They will help you grow in your faith and learn to study the Bible. Plus, Jesus commands us to make a profession of faith. By taking the first step in obeying this command of Jesus, you are showing that your life is different, that you no longer live in darkness, that you are a follower of the Light.

EMERGING ENDEAVORS

Have you ever made a decision to follow Christ? If not, what is holding you back from surrendering your life?

Imagine yourself at the end of your life. What kind of things will be important then? What endeavors might seem unimportant then?

Have you ever told anyone that you are a follower of Christ; that you have emerged from darkness to walk in light? If not, tell someone about your decision.

DAILY TAKEAWAY

FROM TODAY'S DEVO -

WRITE SOMETHING DOWN.

_____

_____

_____

_____

_____

_____

PRAY SOMETHING THROUGH.

_____

_____

_____

_____

_____

PASS SOMETHING ALONG.

_____

_____

_____

_____

_____

_____

DAY 2 **emerge from:**

The Chains of
Insecurity

"I praise you because I am fearfully and wonderfully made; your works are wonderful, I know that full well."

- Psalm 139:14

The Dictionary defines insecurity as "self-doubt or lack of confidence." Do those words describe how you feel about yourself? If so, you are not alone! Over 71% of teens report that they are generally not happy with themselves. This period of your life is often marked with a sense of vulnerability toward others that, if not addressed, can cause you to disengage and withdraw to the prison of your private world.

But remember, every teenager faces insecurity from time to time.

In order to tackle this insecurity, you will have to find your worth in the person God has made you to be. Colossians 1:16 reads, "All things were created by him and for him." Since He created you, God knows your true identity. He knows your real name.

Consider the story of Nebuchadnezzar in the first chapter of Daniel. The Babylonians conquered the city of Jerusalem, and King Nebuchadnezzar ordered the strongest and brightest to serve him in the royal palace. As they joined the king's staff, they were all given Babylonian names. Daniel was called Belteshazzar while Hananiah was called Shadrach, Mishael called Meshach, and Azariah called Abednego.

But check out verse 8. Daniel determined not to defile himself by following the King and not to define himself by his worldly name. His given name, Daniel, translates to "God is my judge," and Daniel stood firm in the name that he knew defined him. His worth was not measured by the fame of being in the King's palace. It was defined by God's definition of him.

Just like Daniel, you were given a name at birth. Maybe you like it. Maybe you don't. Perhaps it has special meaning, or perhaps it just sounds good with your last name. We all have a name that was given to us by the people who love us. However, when we surrender to Christ, we receive a new name.

In John 3:3, Jesus said you must be born again to enter the kingdom of heaven. And 2 Corinthians 5:17 reminds us that we are a new creation. Old things have passed away and all things have been made new. If you have been born again in Christ, you have the privilege of a new identity. At the core of your being, you are new.

The Vietnamese people take this new identity in Christ literally. When someone becomes a Christian in Vietnam, they are given a new Christian name.

Now, I am not suggesting you should march down to the social security building and officially change your given name. I am reminding you that if you have surrendered to Christ, your identity is new. Your insecurity, self-doubt, and anxiety are replaced with peace, strength, truth, comfort, and acceptance.

Your new name is child of God, and nothing can shake the soul anchored to this truth.

EMERGING ENDEAVORS

If you could change your name to anything, what would it be? Why?

Read the list of names that are given to you in Christ. Put a check by at least three that speak to you.

I am loved. (1 John 3:1)

I am accepted. (Ephesians 1:6)

I am a child of God. (John 1:12)

I am Jesus' friend. (John 15:14)

I am a joint heir with Jesus, sharing in His inheritance. (Romans 8:17)

I am a temple of God. His Spirit and his life live in me. (1 Corinthians 6:19)

I am a member of Christ's body. (1 Corinthians 12:27)

I am complete in Jesus Christ. (Colossians 2:10)

I am free from condemnation. (Romans 8:1)

I am a new creation. (2 Corinthians 5:17)

I am chosen by God. I am holy and dearly loved. (Colossians 3:12)

I have a spirit of power, love, and sound mind. (2 Timothy 1:7)

I am God's co-worker. (2 Corinthians 6:1)

I have direct access to God. (Ephesians 2:18)

I can always know the presence of God because He never leaves me. (Hebrews 13:5)

Read the list above everyday for a month, preferably out loud. As you discover your identity in Christ, your confidence will break free from the chains of insecurity.

DAILY TAKEAWAY

FROM TODAY'S DEVO -

WRITE SOMETHING DOWN.

_____
_____
_____
_____
_____

PRAY SOMETHING THROUGH.

_____
_____
_____
_____
_____

PASS SOMETHING ALONG.

_____
_____
_____
_____
_____

The Weight of Pride

"All of you, clothe yourselves with humility toward one another because, 'God opposes the proud but gives grace to the humble.'"

- 1 Peter 5:5

I overheard the following conversation recently, and it made me laugh. A young man tried to gain the attention of a young lady by saying, "Do you believe in love at first sight, or do I need to walk by again?" I found myself shaking me head in disbelief. First, I felt sorry for this poor boy because he was not going to get a date. And second, I was shocked by his pride.

According to Scripture, one sin that hold us down is pride. The Bible clearly states, "Pride goes before destruction, a haughty spirit before a fall." Proverbs 16:18. This mandate from Proverbs gives us the distinction between feeling confident and becoming arrogant.

Arrogance is marked by a feeling of invincibility. On the days when your hair is perfect and your skin is smooth, you might begin to feel like you are hot stuff. It only takes one fall down the stairs, one wrong answer in Chemistry class, or one spilled drink in the cafeteria to bring you back down to reality. Truthfully, our personal confidence fluctuates with the ups and downs of each day, but God gives us a better way.

He says to resist the lure of pride.

Why?

We see prideful athletes, actors, actresses, and politicians who seem to have all the answers.

Just wait. Pride comes before a fall.

When someone is filled with pride, they are not open to advice; they are always right; they are blinded by their own greatness. Decisions are based upon nothing else but to satisfy the desire for power, pleasure, or possessions. Unfortunately, when a person falls into this trap there is no escape except from the pit from which they fall.

The story is almost a cliché in our country. We see the wealthy, prideful business owner declaring bankruptcy. We witness the arrogant athlete stumble into embarrassing trouble. We make jokes about the Hollywood star that was too prideful to see it all crumbling around her.

In James, we are reminded that God resists the proud. So, what does it mean to be proud? It does not mean being confident. It is just what you have confidence in - that is the difference. Confidence in the flesh is the epitome of pride. Confidence in Christ is the epitome of the Christian faith. Christ has the ability and the desire to live through us on a daily basis. My confidence in Christ is what sustains me. It also gives us hope.

I Peter 5:6 reads, "Humble yourself...under Gods mighty hand and in due time he will exalt you." When we surrender to God's authority in our life, we are released to be exalted. This term, "exalted", does not mean that we will shoot the winning goal, or be recognized as the most popular. Peter is referring to the day in which Christ appears. We will be recognized by the One who matters most.

So on this day, let's emerge from the weight of pride and the pursuit of being recognized by this world. Let's humble ourselves now in order to be exalted later.

EMERGING ENDEAVORS

How do you know if you are living under the weight of pride? Can you think of any areas in life where you have become arrogant?

Pray that God will give you grace and humility to seek His will and stay open to His leading. Pray for forgiveness for the prideful areas in your heart.

DAILY TAKEAWAY

FROM TODAY'S DEVO -

WRITE SOMETHING DOWN.

_____
_____
_____
_____
_____
_____

PRAY SOMETHING THROUGH.

_____
_____
_____
_____
_____

PASS SOMETHING ALONG.

_____
_____
_____
_____
_____

emerge from:

The Shackles of Unforgiveness

"Bear with each other and forgive one another if any of you has a grievance against someone. Forgive as the Lord forgave you. And over all these virtues put on love, which binds them all together in perfect unity."

- Colossians 3:13-14

It has been said, "Unforgiveness is like a drinking a deadly poison and hoping the other person dies." I experienced a taste of this firsthand in Junior High School. My family life was rough after my parents divorced, and I felt a heaviness on my heart and mind. Since I did not know how to forgive my parents, I began withdrawing into a shell, refusing to talk to anyone about the pain I felt.

Well, apparently, holding this pain inside caught up with me. It all began with a simple cough, which at first felt like nothing more than an irritated throat, but it worsened into uncontrollable hacking. Soon, I was coughing so continuously that my mom whisked me off to the emergency room.

As we got closer and closer to the hospital, the coughing began to subside. I realized that the stress had been so intense, it manifested into coughing. I had built up unforgiveness in my thoughts, so the only way for my body to deal with it was to release it through coughing. I was slightly embarrassed and surprised that my negative thoughts could turn into physical pain.

I wish I could say this trip to the emergency room was a turning point in my life, but unfortunately that was just a speed bump on a highway of issues that I was dealing with at that time. It wasn't until several years later when I fully surrendered my life to Christ that the healing process actually began. In one amazing night at a youth camp, God removed years of pain and hurt as I cried out at the altar for his help to assist me to move on from my pain. That night, the burden was lifted and I began walking down my path towards forgiving those who had hurt me.

I learned that forgiveness is a process that you have to go through daily. Everyday, you have the opportunity to wake up and "forgive as the Lord has forgiven you." This is where our healing begins.

As you read my story, maybe you are thinking of a person you need to forgive. It could be a family member, friend, teacher, or even an acquaintance. It's possible that this person has no idea you are harboring resentment or anger toward them. I challenge you to bring that pain to the altar and allow God to release you from the chains of unforgiveness.

Don't worry if you feel overwhelmed by the thought of forgiving someone in your life. God promises that He will shoulder your burden. It's okay if you don't know how He will do it. Just trust me. He can. He will.

Release yourself from the chains of unforgiveness and live in the freedom God wants to give you.

EMERGING ENDEAVORS

Who are some people that you are struggling to forgive? If you cannot think of anyone, pray that God will reveal any resentment or unresolved grudges you are holding against people in your life.

Define what they have done to wrong you. Do they even realize that they have hurt you?

Ask God to show you how to begin the process of forgiving and healing. If you are still unsure how to proceed, talk to a trusted advisor, like a youth leader, pastor, or family member.

DAILY TAKEAWAY

FROM TODAY'S DEVO -

WRITE SOMETHING DOWN.

_____

_____

_____

_____

_____

_____

PRAY SOMETHING THROUGH.

_____

_____

_____

_____

_____

_____

PASS SOMETHING ALONG.

_____

_____

_____

_____

_____

_____

emerge from:

The Grip
of Your Friends

"Whoever acknowledges me before others, I will also acknowledge before my Father in heaven. But whoever disowns me before others, I will disown before my Father in heaven."

- Matthew 10:32, 33

When I was fifteen years old, our family moved to a new area and I was desperate to make friends. I was a new Christian, and my life was complicated enough as I tried to rectify my new faith with the daily pressures of being a teenager. I knew God was real to me, and that my commitment to Christ did not come out of tradition or pressure from my family. I knew I had given my life to Christ and that He was the missing puzzle piece in my life.

I knew where I was with God, but I did not know where to fit in at my new school.

The first people I met were the guys on the football team. One day, I drove my scooter to a teammate's house to practice passing routes, when I saw something encouraging in their front yard. His family placed three massive white crosses in the front of the house. I was ecstatic! I had never seen anyone be so bold with his or her faith. I felt this was a sign that these people were here to encourage me in my new walk with God. What I expected to be encouragement turned out to be the first test in standing up against peer pressure. That day, I wasn't the only person who showed up to play a little football. Other kids were there, too, and one of them began using the cross as a backboard, banging the football irreverently against it in defiance. This led to guys taking turns hurling the ball at the crosses, like a target.

It got worse. Some of the guys even climbed on it and mocked Jesus' death. I was shocked that even Christians joined in the mockery. As I watched this display, my heart started racing. I knew the football would be handed to me. What would I do? Would I join in and make fun of all that Jesus had done for me?

I can still feel the leather on my hands as if it were yesterday. I held the ball and had to make a decision. Would I follow my friends or follow Christ? Would I act like Jesus wasn't my Savior in order to fit in with some new friends?

I really wanted friends.

I stared at the ball, and then raised my eyes to the cross. It was the moment of truth. I dropped the ball.

One of the younger kids looked at me and asked, "Aren't you going to do it, too?"

I responded with the first thing that popped into my head. "I'm not stupid." Even though I only had a basic understanding of Jesus, I knew that He was more important than what these guys thought. I chose to honor Jesus first. It might seem like a small act of obedience, but it was huge for me. It was the moment when I decided that other people do not own me. Other people will not tell me what to do.

Jesus was in charge. And He still is.

EMERGING ENDEAVORS

Can you think of a time when other people have encouraged you to do something against the will of God? Did you stand up for what you believe of did you give in?

What type of peer pressure do you feel on a regular basis? Do you feel pressure to gossip, drink, cuss, lie, cheat, or steal?

What are some tangible steps you can do to take a stand for God with your friends?

DAILY TAKEAWAY

FROM TODAY'S DEVO -

WRITE SOMETHING DOWN.

_____
_____
_____
_____
_____
_____

PRAY SOMETHING THROUGH.

_____
_____
_____
_____
_____
_____

PASS SOMETHING ALONG.

_____
_____
_____
_____
_____
_____

"Anyone who loves their father or mother more than me is not worthy of me; anyone who loves their son or daughter more than me is not worthy of me. Whoever does not take up their cross and follow me is not worthy of me. Whoever finds their life will lose it, and whoever loses their life for my sake will find it."

- Matthew 10:37-38

I had to make a decision that summer. I could not deny that God was leading me, and I knew it was a powerful call. For half of my life, I grew up in a neighborhood that was economically depressed, and I felt a passion to go back to the same type of neighborhood and share what God had done for me.

My first mission trip opportunity was not to a third world country or an impoverished nation. It was an opportunity to go back to the city where I was born, to go back to Miami. Every summer my church was part of an outreach to Miami, and I desperately wanted to go, but I had one major hurdle to jump. My mother and stepfather were against it. They felt it was too dangerous for a sixteen-year-old boy to hang out in the projects. Although I was disappointed, I knew it was best to honor my parents. I did not go on the mission trip, but I prayed for the team who went.

At the age of eighteen, I had the opportunity to go again. Since I was older, I did not need parental consent to join the team, but I talked to my stepfather about it anyway. His reaction was not what I wanted to hear. He basically told me that I had gone overboard with all this church stuff, and he thought I was brainwashed!

He drew a line in the sand; he told me to choose.

"Who do you love more, your God or your family?" His words echoed powerfully in my head along with the words of Jesus. "If any man will come after me, he must take up his cross and follow me."

With tears in my eyes, I answered, "I love my family, but I love God more."

"Well, you can go then," he said as he turned and walked out of the room.

21

The dispute left me with mixed emotions. I was upset about arguing with my stepfather, but satisfied that I chose to put Christ first. And even though it was difficult, I know now that it was the right decision. That summer in Miami was life changing for me. It was the first time I ever rapped in front of an audience. It marked the beginning of my inner-city ministry. And God used it to change the entire trajectory of my career.

I wish I could say that my relationship with my stepfather improved, but it got worse. In fact, I eventually moved out because the stress was so severe.

Years later, I entered full-time inner-city ministry with a church in my hometown. The summer I spent in Miami prepared me for the challenges I faced there and later, the challenges of music ministry. Eventually, my stepfather apologized as he witnessed my success and began to understand my heart.

It was not easy to follow God's will over my parents' that summer. It is never easy to go against the desires of people who care about you. But it's during these times that our faith grows and God weaves his purpose in us.

EMERGING ENDEAVORS

What are some pressures that your family places on you? How do those pressures make you feel?

How can you make steps to honor your parent(s)?

What steps can you take to make sure God is honored first in your life and family?

DAILY TAKEAWAY

FROM TODAY'S DEVO -

WRITE SOMETHING DOWN.

_____
_____
_____
_____
_____
_____

PRAY SOMETHING THROUGH.

_____
_____
_____
_____
_____
_____

PASS SOMETHING ALONG.

_____
_____
_____
_____
_____
_____

⊙

EMERGE FROM:

Solitary Confinement

"Be strong and courageous. Do not be afraid or terrified because of them, for the Lord your God goes with you; he will never leave you nor forsake you."

- Deuteronomy 31:6

In 1969, Three Dog Night sang, "One is the loneliest number that you'll ever see." And still today, we can relate to this idea. It does not matter if you are the most successful, most popular, or most gorgeous person in your group, you could still be the loneliest. Wikipedia defines loneliness as "an unpleasant feeling in which a person feels a strong sense of emptiness resulting from inadequate levels of social relationships."

Loneliness is much more than being by oneself. Sometimes I like being alone. It helps me think, plan, and rest. This is called solitude. The Bible tells us that Jesus valued his time alone with God. In Matthew 14, Jesus departed from the crowd to be alone. It was a time of prayer, reflection, and communion with the Father. When was the last time you enjoyed a time of true solitude?

Ironically, you will best emerge from loneliness by understanding the strength in solitude.

Most people advise you to overcome loneliness by staying busy and surrounding yourself with people. I disagree. You can be in a crowded room and still feel alone. So, how can you escape the pangs of loneliness?

First, focus on the relationship that matters most. Start with Jesus. I know it sounds elementary, but have you considered that Christianity is not a fairy tale and your relationship with Jesus is real? I understand you cannot see or hear Him, but you can sense His presence. Invite His presence to fill your heart. Trust in His Word that He will never leave nor forsake you. Understand that He has plans to prosper you and not harm you.

Second, fuel your energy towards making an impact. Instead of focusing on your personal void, seek to fill the void in others. Fix a meal for a neighbor. Sit with someone who looks lonely. Encourage a friend who is struggling. Your goal is not to stay busy but to do something that makes an impact. Busyness is bound to lead to loneliness while thoughtfulness leads to fulfillment.

Third, find an opportunity to serve. It could be a homeless shelter, an elderly home, or the humane society, but find a place where you can make a difference. Remember, as you are serving, it's not about activity. It's about making an impact and doing it for the Lord. Colossians 3:23 reads, "Whatever you do, do it with all your heart, as working for the Lord, not men." This is the key to living without loneliness. Surrender every action to the will of God.

Fourth, know that you matter. Whenever you doubt your worth, read Psalm 139.

Check out an excerpt from this chapter in the Bible that reminds us that God is always with us.

For you created my inmost being;
you knit me together in my mother's womb.
I praise you because I am fearfully and wonderfully made;
your works are wonderful,
I know that full well.
My frame was not hidden from you
when I was made in the secret place,
when I was woven together in the depths of the earth.
Your eyes saw my unformed body;
all the days ordained for me were written in your book
before one of them came to be.
How precious to me are your thoughts, oh God!
How vast is the sum of them!
Were I to count them, they would outnumber the grains of sand—
when I awake, I am still with you.

The Psalmist remembers that God was with him in the beginning of his life. God is with you now. You are never alone. Seek strength in solitude with the One who knows you like no one else does. He understands your past, cares about your present, and directs your future.

EMERGING ENDEAVORS

How often do you feel lonely? Where and when do you feel overwhelmed by loneliness?

Are you comfortable spending time alone, in quiet solitude? For the next ten minutes, turn off all electronic devices. Go to a quiet place and breathe deeply. Focus on listening and talking to God without distractions and sense the strength that comes in solitude with Jesus.

Can you think of anyone in your life who might be lonely? Pray for them. Then, send them a text to let them know that you are thinking of them.

DAILY TAKEAWAY

FROM TODAY'S DEVO -

WRITE SOMETHING DOWN.

_____

_____

_____

_____

_____

_____

PRAY SOMETHING THROUGH.

_____

_____

_____

_____

_____

PASS SOMETHING ALONG.

_____

_____

_____

_____

_____

_____

"A gossip betrays a confidence, but a trustworthy man keeps a secret."

- Proverbs 11:13

Gossip is defined as slanderous conversation or words that do not edify another person. Although we often hide gossip under a mask of concern, it's time to remove the masks. It's time to clean up our conversations.

Gossip has no place in the life of someone attempting to make an impact for the Kingdom of God. Although we know that unwholesome talk ruins our witness, why has this sin infiltrated the Church? Is it possible that we have allowed it into our lives because we consider it a small sin? Be warned. God does not take gossip lightly. Paul tells us that slanderers cause the judgment of God to fall upon the nations, and he mentions slander along with murder on the list of sins God hates.

Once we are aware of God's view of gossip, we need to examine our own motive for talking about people, often people we love. One motive for gossip is a low self-image. By tearing others down, these gossipers feel better about themselves. Other people gossip in order to cause pain. And still others gossip out of the need to be liked. But using gossip to cure your own insecurity will never work. In the end, you lose respect for yourself and others lose respect for you as well.

If you notice the sin of gossip creeping into your life, do not walk; run from it. Here are three ways to run from gossip. First, confess to the person you have slandered. I know that is the LAST thing you want to do, but trust me; you will gain more respect through honest confession than you will ever find trying to cover up your words. Plus, if you know you will have to confess every time you gossip, I guarantee you will think twice the next time you hear a morsel of juicy gossip. Second, ask God to forgive you and protect your tongue.

James warns us about the danger of the tongue. "Understand this, my dear brothers and sisters! Let every person be quick to listen, slow to speak, slow to anger. For human anger does not accomplish God's righteousness. If someone thinks he is religious yet does not bridle his tongue, and so deceives his heart, his religion is futile." James 1:19-20, 26

Why would God call our religion futile if we cannot control our tongue? We find the answer in Matthew 12:34, "Out of the overflow of the heart, the mouth speaks." Your words reveal what is in your heart. That's scary! When you catch yourself tearing down your friend, you are revealing the sin in your own heart.

So, if you are struggling with the serious sin of gossip, it might be a wake-up call about the need to confess and spend time with God. You have a choice. You can continue to live by the standards of the world, looking out for number one, tearing others down, and speaking words of the gutter, or you can ask God to help you speak His words.

It's your choice.

I encourage you to turn toward Christ, and let your speech reflect something better than slanderous gossip. Ephesians 4:29 reads, "Do not let any unwholesome talk come out of your mouth, but only what is helpful for building others up, according to their need, that what you say will benefit those who hear."

Let Ephesians 4:29 be your guide. Before sharing information ask yourself three questions: 1.) Is this true? 2.) Is it helpful? 3.) Is it necessary? When you can't decide if your speech is wholesome, put it to the test. Only say it if it's true, helpful, and necessary.

When others know that you are the kind of person who speaks truth, who uplifts, and who only shares what is necessary, they will be able to trust you when it counts. They trust you when you share God's Word. They trust you when they need to talk to someone because their life is falling apart. They trust you enough to open up and tell you their pain.

And this is the bridge of trust that must be built in order to be a faithful witness.

EMERGING ENDEAVORS

What are the reasons why you have gossiped in the past? How can you avoid repeating the same mistakes again?

Take time to pray for your tongue. Pray that God will control it so you can be a faithful witness among your friends.

DAILY TAKEAWAY

FROM TODAY'S DEVO -

WRITE SOMETHING DOWN.

_____
_____
_____
_____
_____
_____

PRAY SOMETHING THROUGH.

_____
_____
_____
_____
_____

PASS SOMETHING ALONG.

_____
_____
_____
_____
_____

A Dead Language

"I said, 'I will watch my ways and keep my tongue from sin...'"

- Psalm 39:1a

Have you ever thought about the size of your tongue? The average male tongue weighs two and a half ounces. For a woman, the average tongue weighs a little over two ounces. That is roughly the weight of a few paperclips.

The tongue is but a small part of the body, but it serves three important functions. First, it allows you to taste your food. Second, it gives your mouth the ability to swallow food. Third, it helps your lips form words so you can speak.

Recently I was in South Africa where the native language is Zulu. It is a language with very fast syllables and rapid clicking of the tongue. I remember one evening, driving in a car with five guys who spoke Zulu, and I could not understand a word they were saying. As I prepared to deliver a message in a remote village, I opened my Bible to James 3: 7 -10. It read, "All kinds of animals, birds, reptiles and sea creatures are being tamed and have been tamed by mankind, but no human being can tame the tongue. It is a restless evil, full of deadly poison. With the tongue we praise our Lord and Father, and with it we curse human beings, who have been made in God's likeness. Out of the same mouth comes praise and cursing. My brothers and sisters, this should not be."

After reading that, I began to wonder if the guys in this car speaking Zulu were praising God with their tongues or cursing human beings, namely me. I even thought, they could be cussing me out and I would never know it.

Those thoughts led me to think about my new native language... not just English, but a cleaner version of English than I used to speak before I knew Christ. 2 Corinthians 5:17 reminds us that when we come to Christ, we are a new creation. This includes our tongue. Our old life, with it's rudeness, sarcasm, and lying, and cussing, is now dead. The new life with encouragement, kindness, and truthfulness is alive in us.

Before He forgave me of all my sins, I was dead in my sins. My spirit was dead and when I spoke; I spoke a dead language. My dead language had nothing to do with glorifying God or sharing the name of Christ. My words were used to draw attention to myself rather than God. I used cuss words to follow others, to get what I wanted, and to destroy people I didn't like.

But that all changed when I accepted the forgiveness of God in Christ Jesus. He cut away that dead language from my tongue and gave me a language that is alive and full of life. Now my new language glorifies Him and is used to bring others out into the world of the living.

But none of us will ever draw people to God using a dead language. Colossians 4:6 says, "Let your conversation be always full of grace, seasoned with salt, so that you may know how to answer everyone." People are looking for life; so let them find it as you speak with kindness and truth rather than profanity.

That night when we arrived at the village, I was told to keep my head down and walk into this tent. When I did, they took my Bible from me and hundreds of villagers began to cheer and shout because the man of God had arrived. They gently laid my Bible on the wooden stand and the translator asked me to step forward and bring the words of life to these people. I am not perfect all the time, but that night my tongue spoke in an ancient language that everyone could understand, the language of God's Love.

EMERGING ENDEAVORS

Think back on your life over the past month. If a survey was sent out about the kind of language you have been using around school, around friends, and even on Facebook, what would they say? Would they say you have been speaking the language of the dead or the living?

Write down all of the words you have ever said in your life that would be considered dead (cuss) words? Once you have written them all down, would you confess those words to God and ask him change your language, to stop chasing cool, and stop giving in to pressure to speak like this?

Now before your parents see this, would you take your pen and scratch out every word and above each one of them, write the name, "Jesus". Pray to God that He would give you the strength to mark those words out of your vocabulary for good.

DAILY TAKEAWAY

FROM TODAY'S DEVO -

WRITE SOMETHING DOWN.

_____

_____

_____

_____

_____

_____

PRAY SOMETHING THROUGH.

_____

_____

_____

_____

_____

PASS SOMETHING ALONG.

_____

_____

_____

_____

_____

"Truthful lips endure forever, but a lying tongue lasts only a moment."

- Proverbs 12:19

Are you a person of your word?

Can people count on you?

I will always be thankful for a dear friend of mine, Dr. Bill. When I was a young man at the start of my ministry, I had a big problem. It was promising things I could not possibly deliver. I justified it by telling myself, "I'm busy. I have so much on my plate. Plus, no one will remember what I promised."

So, Dr. Bill invited me to lunch to set me straight. He basically said, "Stop it. You are killing your long-term witness for Christ. People must know they can trust you." It felt like a dagger through my heart. I wanted to turn and run, but I couldn't. I had to face the fact that this was a form of lying.

In fact, lying can take many forms. There is the exaggeration, the little white lie, the lie of omission (which means omitting important information). However, if we are going to emerge from the shadows, we must understand how to stand on truth.

Proverbs 12:22 reads, "The Lord detests lying lips, but he delights in men who are truthful." The word, "detest" means "hate." God does not hate people, but He does hate certain actions. In Proverbs 6, we read that lying lips are part of the seven things God hates. In order to emerge from the shadows we must remove lying from our lives... in all its forms.

I am forever grateful for my friend who spoke truth in my life. Another friend tells me he looks for people who will do two things. First, they tell him what they are going to do. Without this piece of information, there is no direction. Second, they do what they say. Without this, there is no integrity.

So, how is your integrity? How is your honesty? Are you like I was at one time? Do you promise things that you can't deliver?

Maybe you tend to exaggerate or tell little white lies. I have an exercise that may help you. Here it is. The next time you lie, you must admit it publicly to the person to whom you lied. WOW! If you commit to this, you may never lie again! In order for this to be successful, you must keep your eyes on the prize. Remember, the Lord delights in people who are truthful.

If you are willing to accept this challenge, tell someone you trust. They will be able to keep you accountable for being a man or woman of truth.

The best thing about becoming a person of absolute truth is that you have nothing to hide. As I write this devotional, there are plenty of stories in the news that can illustrate this point, but none are as serious as the Penn State controversy in 2011. A coach that won over 400 football games, who led a storied Division I University, who set records and built a legacy found himself in the middle of a mess.

And why was Joe Paterno in the middle of the mess? Not because he was guilty of abusing young children, but because he did not speak the truth. He did not necessarily lie, but he did not SPEAK the whole truth.

As we emerge and engage we must learn that NOT LYING is NOT GOOD ENOUGH. We must speak the truth.

EMERGING ENDEAVORS

Can you think of the last lie you told? What were the circumstances, and why did you decide to deceive?

On a scale of 1 to 10, how difficult do you think it would be to remove deception from your life? Would you be willing to commit to becoming a person of absolute truth?

How do you think little white lies, exaggeration, and lies of omission affect your witness for Christ?

DAILY TAKEAWAY

FROM TODAY'S DEVO -

WRITE SOMETHING DOWN.

_____

_____

_____

_____

_____

PRAY SOMETHING THROUGH.

_____

_____

_____

_____

_____

PASS SOMETHING ALONG.

_____

_____

_____

_____

_____

The Enticement of Impurity

"I made a covenant with my eyes not to look lustfully at a girl."

– Job 31:1

Imagine yourself, standing in a crowd of friends at school, when suddenly someone shouts your name. In front of everyone, they yell, "Dude, check out these pics on my phone! This girl is totally naked!" Most likely, you would walk away. Why? Because you would be embarrassed to have your friends see you look at naked pictures. Although you might check out the pictures alone, it seems dirty when confronted with nakedness in front of other people.

It's a fact. We are ashamed of nakedness – our own and the nakedness of others. We like to be covered; we like our privacy.

If you don't believe me, check out the embarrassment on the kid's face when his pants are pulled down during gym class. Or listen to the person scream when you accidentally open their stall in the bathroom.

The shame we all feel about nakedness began in the Garden of Eden. Before sin entered the world, Adam and Eve "were both naked and they felt no shame," Genesis 2:25. But when they disobeyed God, and sin entered the world, their first action was to cover themselves. Suddenly, they were not comfortable with complete intimacy and vulnerability.

Have you ever considered the fact that humans are the only species that notice their nakedness? You never see a zookeeper hide the animals while they get dressed. Your dog does not screech, "Turn your head! I have to put my jeans on!" He never says that because he's a dog. He's an animal.

Unfortunately, our culture sends the message that humans are nothing more than animals, and nakedness is not sacred to the marriage bed. According to the media and popular culture, humans might as well sleep in doggie beds. We are just like the animals. And this prevailing attitude has created a world rampant with pornography, sexual immorality, and uncontrolled lust.

The trappings of this culture leave humans feasting on dog food and sleeping in dog beds.

My dog does not go, "Oh, turn your head! Let me put my gym shorts on!" No. He's a dog, an animal. But our culture says we're a bunch of animals. So, if we're animals, we should act like animals and treat other people like an animal, doing what we want and wherever we want. The culture says we should just sleep in our doggie beds instead of the marriage bed because that's what sex is. We're not humans. We're just animals.

Our animal instinct continues to feed the pornography industry as it is estimated that the world spends over $3,000 per second on porn. Ephesians 4:19 reads, "Having lost all sensitivity, they have given themselves over to sensuality so as to indulge in every kind of impurity, with a continual lust for more." By giving into these sinful instincts, we are setting ourselves up to be continually trapped by unfulfilled longings. The world says, "This is the way to fulfill your needs," but God knows it's a trap, and He shows us a better way.

God, though, says sex is for the marriage bed. A husband and wife making love, is reflecting the nature and the character of God. So God thought up sex. It was his idea. It was given to us before sin ever entered the human equation. We will never discover the mystery and the beauty and the depth of sex until we do it God's way. It will not occur in your life or mine until we say, "Okay, God, I'm going to do sex your way."

Emerge from the doggie beds of the world and fight for your marriage bed one day. Push back from the dog food buffet and pull up to the table of God. If you are struggling in this area, I promise you, your youth pastor or leader can help you pray through it. They want to help you emerge from this lie in your life.

Read 1 Peter 1:18-19. If you feel that you have done too much, that you have destroyed your worth in this area, I want you to remember this verse. You were bought with a price and your Heavenly Father paid for you with blood of His very own son. You are worth more than you know to God.

Would you confess right now you are struggling in this area? Would you confess that this area is a sin and you need God's forgiveness? (1 John 1:9) Stop right now, pray from your heart, and lay this down at the feet of Jesus.

Commit today that you are going to save yourself from this day forward for the wonderful sex that God has waiting for you in your future.

DAILY TAKEAWAY

FROM TODAY'S DEVO -

WRITE SOMETHING DOWN.

_____
_____
_____
_____
_____
_____

PRAY SOMETHING THROUGH.

_____
_____
_____
_____
_____

PASS SOMETHING ALONG.

_____
_____
_____
_____
_____
_____

DAY 12

emerge from:

Pursuing False Pleasures

"I said to myself, 'Come now, I will test you with pleasure to find out what is good.' But that also proved to be meaningless."

- Ecclesiastes 2:1

America has it all, doesn't she? Food. Entertainment. Games. Clothes. Movies. Shoes. Where else but America can you find a fast food restaurant next door to a fast weight loss clinic?

We live in a world that screams, "You need a little bit more!" One more pair of sunglasses. Just a little bit more money. A faster car. A sweeter vacation. Commercials, billboards, and pop-up ads remind you to live for yourself. You can have it all! You deserve it! You are inundated with the mindset to live selfishly.

However, a life pursuing only selfish interests offers little hope. It is like a cloudy day without rain. You carry your umbrella all day, but the drops never fall. So many people live their life expecting peace to come through the pursuit of pleasure, only to find it never comes.

The secret to real peace is found in what Jesus tells us in John 12:24. In order to have life, we must die. We must die to our selfishness. The good news found in Romans is that we have been "baptized into the death of Christ." This means that if you truly know Jesus, you are already dead! Jesus took your sin and the penalty and your former life is gone.

That's the good news. Now, here is the bad. In order to walk in this abundant life, we must stay dead. Allow me to explain. In 1 Corinthians, Paul writes, "I die daily..." What does this mean to you and me? It means that we must choose who directs our lives each day. It's either Christ or me.

So, who is in charge of your life today?

Just because you died to self yesterday does not mean you are dead today. When you are at a church retreat, you may be Mr. or Ms. Walking Dead Man for Jesus, but how about it when you forget your homework? How dead are you when the referee makes a bad call? We are constantly challenged to die to momentary pleasures and seek God's greater purpose.

Sometimes our decision to die to self is not obvious. It's not a flashing neon sign that reads, "Good versus Evil." Instead, it's a seemingly insignificant moment during a regular Tuesday when we have to decide between good and best.

For me, the gross, immoral, and indulgent sin is not that difficult to resist. It's the small stuff... like a hot fudge sundae or the seventh cup of coffee after a hectic day that gets me. It could be the tiniest morsel of gossip or the guilty pleasure of a television show that does not glorify God that draws you away from God's best.

Of course, all fun is not a sin! Every ice cream cone is not forbidden for Christians, but anything that controls you or takes your focus off your mission is sin. Ask yourself, "Does this impede my walk with Christ?" Be honest as you answer that question with gray areas in your life.

Remember, life is not about what you can get, but who you can give. With this reasoning, vacation is not sin. Candy is not a sin. But when the pursuit of such pleasures controls your motives, it's time to make a change. When a possession becomes an obsession, give it away. When caffeine becomes more important than your quiet time, toss out the Diet Coke. Do not release control of your emotions to anyone but Christ.

Ponder these questions today. What is my pursuit in life? What are the areas of my life that have made my pursuit of Jesus foggy or diluted? What would I be willing to give up in this world for my walk in Christ? I hope you say everything. Our goal in life is to be a workman approved for his service. Let's emerge from the pursuit of stuff and engage our communities with the truth that Jesus is better than anything on earth.

EMERGING ENDEAVORS

What fears do you have about completely dying to self and giving Christ full reign over the smallest details of your life?

On an average day, what distracts you from walking closely with God?

What pursuits should you turn over to God?

DAILY TAKEAWAY

FROM TODAY'S DEVO -

WRITE SOMETHING DOWN.

_____

_____

_____

_____

_____

PRAY SOMETHING THROUGH.

_____

_____

_____

_____

_____

PASS SOMETHING ALONG.

_____

_____

_____

_____

_____

emerge From:
The Vultures of Culture

"Do not conform any longer to the pattern of this world, but be transformed by the renewing of your mind. Then you will be able to test and approve what God's will is–his good, pleasing and perfect will."

- Romans 12:2

My youngest son is four years old, and it takes two grown-ups to keep up with him. We usually know that something bad is about to happen when we hear... nothing. Silence is the signal that he has found trouble.

My wife will say, "Do you hear anything?"

And I'll respond, "Yeah, it's way too quiet. Where is he?"

One night, my wife noticed the silence, so she began searching the house. She could not find him anywhere. Finally, he walked out the bathroom with a swagger, like he had done something really cool. By the way, he was chewing on something. He was gnawing on THE TOILET BRUSH!! And not a new one, either. He had one that had been around a while.

When asked why he was chewing on the crusty, yellow brush, he said, "Because it's fuzzy!" Insane. I know. He doesn't realize he's feasting on poop, but I venture to say we feast on poop regularly. As a culture, we chew up disgusting bits of whatever the media throws out via television, magazines, movies, and YouTube.

But teenagers, let me remind you that YOU have more power than you realize. You are the ones who buy the new shoes, who watch the videos on YouTube, who flock to the latest vampire movie. Without you, there is no culture.

Unfortunately, many young people use culture as their Bible, their guiding standard for what is right and wrong, what is good and bad, what is best for their lives. Popular culture defines how they spend their money and what is important to them. Culture, if left unchecked, will define an entire value system.

It is not uncommon for me to talk to a teenager who doesn't believe in God simply because they read an article in some teen magazine. Sex, abortion, and homosexuality are widely accepted because culture has redefined them. We are evolving and the god of Culture is leading us there. 2 Corinthians 4:4 reads, "The god of this age has blinded the minds of unbelievers, so that they cannot see the light of the gospel of the glory of Christ, who is the image of God."

The god of this age is our popular culture, and it is blinding those who become its followers. By following the god of culture, we will miss out on everything our Father in Heaven created life to be. Remember, God thought of this life. It was His idea! His image and creativity is woven into the very framework and fabric of our existence.

His best creative work, however, was you. Your physical uniqueness is evident in the sound of your voice, the uniqueness of your fingerprints, and even the intricacy of your eyes. No two people have the same intellectual capacity, emotional makeup, experiences, gifts, and passions. You have the image of God all over you. You are His masterpiece!

And God not only designed you with great care, but He also lovingly gave you His Word to guide you through this life. Probably the greatest most thoughtful gift God has ever given to us, next to the blood of His son, is the love letter He wrote called the Bible. In it you will find His thoughts about you as He was creating you in His image. In it you will find the answers to the deepest mysteries of life. You will find the acceptance and belonging your heart so desperately desires.

Emerge from the world of culture and let the Word of God redefine who you are in Christ.

EMERGING ENDEAVORS

If you are in your room while you are doing this devotion, look around your room and ask yourself this question, "How much of my room has been defined by culture and how much has been defined by God?"

Write verses you have learned about in this book onto cards and display them in your room. What else could you do to transform your room to glorify God more?

Ask yourself, what needs change to make my life look more like Christ and less like culture? What areas need to be redefined by God for you?

DAILY TAKEAWAY

FROM TODAY'S DEVO -

WRITE SOMETHING DOWN.

_____
_____
_____
_____
_____
_____

PRAY SOMETHING THROUGH.

_____
_____
_____
_____
_____
_____

PASS SOMETHING ALONG.

_____
_____
_____
_____
_____
_____

Noise Pollution

"He says, 'Be still, and know that I am God;
I will be exalted among the nations,
I will be exalted in the earth.'"

- **Psalm 46:10**

The word noise comes from the Latin word, nauseous, which means "seasickness". This is due to the fact that both nausea and noise cause some type of unwanted discomfort.

If the noise is unwanted, like a car stereo resounding through a quiet neighborhood, then the law considers it noise pollution. They say a sound may be considered noise pollution if it disturbs any natural process or causes human disruption, i.e. sleep.

Although construction, music, airplanes, or trains generally cause noise pollution, I would say that we all endure other types of unwanted noise in our daily lives, too. Cell phones, commercials, telemarketers, fire alarms, and even Facebook messages interrupt us. If we are not careful, our attention can be hijacked by the constant noise pollution.

Culture has trained our ears to pay attention to the loudest and flashiest information while ignoring what is important. Like a radio that is tuned into the wrong station, we are tuned to hear the noise rather than the Holy Spirit.

It's time to change stations.

God knew that we would have to make an effort to hear what is important. Maybe that is why the phrase, "He who has ears, let him hear," appears in the Bible fourteen times!

Think about this. When you pick up your phone (assuming you did not check caller ID), how long does it take you recognize the voice on the other end? If you know the person well, you recognize their voice almost instantly. This is because each person's voice is unique. It has a distinct tone based on the size of your vocal cavities, mouth, and teeth. This means your voiceprint is much like a fingerprint... no two are alike. In the future, you might log into your computer just using the sound of your voice. Crime scene investigators are even using new technology to catch criminals based on voiceprint technology. Scary, huh?

Ask yourself these questions. Do you recognize God's voiceprint? Are your ears tuned into His station? How long does it take you to know when God is talking to you?

John 10:27 reads, "My sheep hear my voice, and I know them, and they follow me." In John 18:37, Jesus says, "Everyone who is of the truth hears my voice."

God is telling us that we do not need voice recognition software to know when He is speaking.

Check out Jesus' words as he explains that, as Christians, we have the ability to hear and know God's voice, even when others do not.

His disciples came and asked him, "Why do you always tell stories when you talk to the people?"

Then he explained to them, "You have been permitted to understand the secrets of the Kingdom of Heaven, but others have not. To those who are open to my teaching, more understanding will be given, and they will have an abundance of knowledge. But to those who are not listening, even what they have will be taken away from them. That is why I tell these stories, because people see what I do, but they don't really see. They hear what I say, but they don't really hear, and they don't understand. This fulfills the prophecy of Isaiah, which says:

"You will hear my words, but you will not understand; you will see what I do, but you will not perceive its meaning. For the hearts of these people are hardened, and their ears cannot hear, and they have closed their eyes- so their eyes cannot see, and their ears cannot hear, and their hearts cannot understand, and they cannot turn to me and let me heal them.'

But blessed are your eyes, because they see; and your ears, because they hear. I assure you, many prophets and godly people have longed to see and hear what you have seen and heard, but they could not." - Matthew 13:10-17

Will you emerge from the noise pollution of culture and engage a God who wants to speak to you to right now?

EMERGING ENDEAVORS

You must want to have eyes that see and have ears that hear. You must desire to have a heart that understands so you can turn to Him. Will you stop right now and pray for God to open your ears so you can understand what He is telling you now?

Go through your life and think of all the things that you would consider noise pollution. Think about anything that would keep you tuned in to the frequencies of the world rather than God. Write them down and commit to one-by-one laying them at the foot of the cross and replacing them with time spent in the Bible.

DAILY TAKEAWAY

FROM TODAY'S DEVO -

WRITE SOMETHING DOWN.

_____

_____

_____

_____

_____

PRAY SOMETHING THROUGH.

_____

_____

_____

_____

_____

PASS SOMETHING ALONG.

_____

_____

_____

_____

_____

Bouts with Doubt

"Then he said to Thomas, 'Put your finger here; see my hands. Reach out your hand and put it into my side. Stop doubting and believe.'"

- John 20:27

What if God gave you a quota on the number of questions you could ask Him? If God informed you that you could only ask two questions, what would they be? Certainly you would pick questions that have been nagging you for years. Maybe you have wondered about how God made the universe, why bad things happen to good people, or exactly when Jesus is coming back.

All of us deal with unanswered questions about life and God.

Author Philip Yancey said, "God's invisibility guarantees I will experience times of doubt." In other words, we all are going to experience bouts with doubt. It's going to happen. We all have questions.

Does God really love me? Can this huge and sovereign God really show his desire for me? Can God forgive me? Can He really wipe the slate clean? Can He really turn his back on the stuff that I have done? How can a good God allow all the pain and the suffering in the world?

And the list goes on. If we are not careful, many of us will allow our doubts to render us useless. We can become paralyzed in our faith because we are struggling with questions that no one can answer perfectly. Many Christians are afraid to emerge from their place of hiding and engage the world with the Gospel because they are afraid of even deeper questions. They go as far as actually believing they are no longer Christians because they have so many questions.

But let me bring good news.

Doubt and unbelief are different animals.

If you are thinking, "I doubt, so it must mean I don't believe", that is not true. Doubt and belief are related; you need them both. The word doubt comes from a Latin term dubitare whose root word is "two." In other words, I am between one and two. I'm kind of hanging there, in limbo.

The word, believe means to be of one mind about something that we trust. To disbelieve, means to lack belief, or to turn my back on something. So, just because I doubt does not mean I don't believe. However, doubt can lead us to unbelief if we don't take our doubts to the One who can teach, instruct, and give faith. When we don't take our questions to God, we give the devil root to tempt us. He says, "Oh, you doubt! That means you don't believe. That means you are not a Christ-follower. That means you don't have any faith."

If every single question were answered, there would be no faith.

Doubt is not a crime against the Word of God. Take John the Baptist as an example. John the Baptist saw Jesus Christ and he said, "There is the Lamb of God." John baptized him. John saw the Holy Spirit descending upon the Lord in the form of a dove. Later, John the Baptist was thrown in prison. It was crunch time. What did he do? He had a bout with doubt. John the Baptist! The baptizer of Jesus, the forerunner of our Lord, the one who witnessed all these miracles, had a bout with doubt.

Luke Chapter 7, Verse 19: "John, while in prison, dispatched some of his friends to go to Christ and ask him, 'Are you the one who was to come or should we expect someone else?'" Look at Christ's response. "Go back and report to John what you have seen and heard. The blind receive sight, the lame walk, those who have leprosy are cured, the deaf hear, the dead are raised, and the good news is preached to the poor."

I love what happens in verse 28; Jesus gave John the Baptist, during a bout with doubt, the ultimate high five. He said, "I tell you among those born of women, there is no one greater than John." Wow! Are you kidding me? Jesus said, "John, you are a great man of faith even though you are in the midst of a bout with doubt."

God is our perfect heavenly parent. He knows that a real relationship requires asking questions and discovering the truth. He wants us to express our doubts, our issues and our concerns to him. He wants us to be His children, and like any child, ask questions as we are growing up!

Don't let your doubts choke your faith; rather let them lead you into a deeper connection and a deeper walk with the Lord. Doubt is not a blockade to spiritual growth. When you take your bouts with doubt to God, He will allow them to strengthen your faith and draw you closer to Him.

We have got to learn how to throw our questions to God because He has never been caught off-guard. Don't let your doubts get you down. An unanswered question is nothing more than an invitation to an adventure in discovering the mysteries of life. So, jump in and let God take your doubts down for the count.

EMERGING ENDEAVORS

The worse thing you can do as a doubter is to doubt in isolation. You need to doubt in a community of people who are seekers of the truth. Write the names of people with whom you might be able to share some of your doubts and questions.

Would you commit to getting them together and writing down the questions you have about God and life and then taking that list of questions to a pastor or youth pastor to help you answer them?

Would pray right now and thank God for his high five to John the Baptist during his bout with doubt and that he wants to do the same for you?

DAILY TAKEAWAY

FROM TODAY'S DEVO -

WRITE SOMETHING DOWN.

_____

_____

_____

_____

_____

_____

PRAY SOMETHING THROUGH.

_____

_____

_____

_____

_____

PASS SOMETHING ALONG.

_____

_____

_____

_____

_____

_____

PART II: ENGAGE

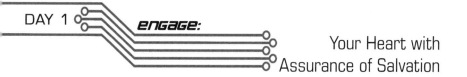

DAY 1 *engage:*

Your Heart with
Assurance of Salvation

"I tell you the truth, whoever hears my word and believes him who sent me has eternal life and will not be condemned; he has crossed over from death to life."

- John 5:24

Should you make decisions based on facts or feelings? Of course, it makes sense to base decisions on facts. Why? Because feelings oscillate up and down like a roller coaster. During times of anxiety or stress, you feel like you're spiraling downward, like a cart on the edge of a rickety track. During good times, you are riding along with the sun on your face, enjoying the smooth track with a smile on your face. But guess what? A big turn is just around the corner! In fact, we might change the way we feel twenty times per day! Our salvation cannot be hitched to such an unstable cart.

As a minister of the gospel, I spend a lot of time dealing with people's feelings concerning their salvation. Of course, you must be saved. John 3 tells us, "You must be born again." But once you are born again, you belong to God, and you can be confident in your salvation.

What are the main reasons people struggle with the idea of losing their salvation? First, they might fall victim to errant theology. If they incorrectly base their salvation on works, they believe they've lost it when their actions are less than perfect. If this is you, remember, you did not earn your salvation in the first place!

Second, some people struggle with past sins and the inability to forgive themselves. They stumble or turn their back on God and then cannot forget this lapse in judgment. If you are struggling to forgive yourself, now is the time to surrender. God has already forgiven you for everything you will ever do. Remember Peter? He denied Jesus three times, and yet, on the resurrection morning, when the women found Jesus at the tomb, He told them, "Go, tell the disciples and Peter..." And when Jesus met Peter on the shore, we see the beautiful view of reconciliation that Christ offers all of us.

His reconciliation is based solely on His love for Peter.

If you are dealing with past sins, first confess the sin to God. Ask Him for forgiveness. Second, believe in the power of forgiveness. Just like an Etch-A-Sketch board erases the stencil when shaken, remember the verse in I John. "If we confess our sin, He is faithful and just to forgive us of our sin and cleanse us from ALL unrighteousness." Third, walk by the fact that Jesus restores and heals. Do not let Satan rob you of tomorrow based on the memories of yesterday.

Third, some people struggle due to simple ignorance. They do not understand the power of salvation. Jesus does not try to change the rules once you come to know Him. He loves you and has a plan for your life. He wants to be instrumental in your decisions and Lord over all. Countless times, I meet with people who "feel" like God does not love them.

As I write this, I am boarding an airplane. I have never met the pilot, and I do not have time to inspect the plane myself. But I have faith that this plane will fly to my destination. I can either be scared to death or walk on that plane with confidence.

How can you get over your concern about salvation? First, remember who saved you. Jesus is faithful and true. He began a good work in you, and He will be faithful to complete it. Second, remember how you were saved. You did nothing for it; you cannot do anything to lose it. However, it did cost Jesus His life. So, live a life of obedience and recognition of the One who loves me.

Finally, remember why He saved you. He loves you more than you love yourself. He simply adores you! Like an adopted child who is loved and adored by his or her parents, you are chosen and perfectly accepted!

The next time you question your salvation, focus outward rather than inward. Look for someone to tell about Jesus, and allow God to work in you and through you.

ENGAGING ENDEAVORS

Do you struggle with doubts about your salvation? Stop and pray that God will give you peace knowing that He is sufficient to save you.

Do you know someone who might struggle with doubts about their salvation? How could you minister to them?

Read Romans 8:38-39. How does God speak to you through these verses?

DAILY TAKEAWAY

FROM TODAY'S DEVO -

WRITE SOMETHING DOWN.

PRAY SOMETHING THROUGH.

PASS SOMETHING ALONG.

"Let the message of Christ dwell among you richly as you teach and admonish one another with all wisdom through psalms, hymns, and songs from the Spirit, singing to God with gratitude in your hearts."

- Colossians 3:16

Do you ever look at God's Word and wonder, "How can I get anything out of this?" We have all been overwhelmed by the idea of studying Scripture, but in order to get something out of it, you must first get into it!

So, what is your excuse?

What hinders you from reading the number one best-selling book of all time? What could possibly be more exciting than hearing from God, more important than gaining pure wisdom, or more meaningful than discovering God's will for your life?

These questions are not meant to invoke guilt, but rather to help you think about why you don't spend more time with such a powerful tool. Check the top three reasons below why you have not studied God's Word as often as you would like.

_____ I don't have time.
_____ I am not sure where to start.
_____ The Bible seems confusing.
_____ I don't believe it will help me.
_____ Scripture is boring.
_____ I don't like to read.
_____ I have too much school work.
_____ I am overwhelmed by the thought of studying the Bible.
_____ I already know basically what it says.
_____ Other _____

Well, today that is going to change. From this moment, you will be able to read any passage of Scripture with an expectation of hearing from God. Whatever your excuse, I challenge you to throw it out and commit to engage God's Word for the next two weeks. God has a plan for your life.

He not only has a plan, He has a growth plan for your life.

You owe it to yourself to discover that plan.

God's Word is alive and promises never to return void. Spending time with Scripture is always a wise investment of your most precious asset: your life. Our burden is to learn HOW to read God's Word, not IF we should read it. Let me teach you a simple method for studying the Bible that removes the guesswork. Whenever you read, ask yourself five questions.

Question 1: Is this passage revealing sin I need to confess?

As you view your life in comparison to God's Word, you will surely feel conviction. Now, God does not want us to live under condemnation, but under a confession. We confess anything that hinders our relationship with Him. So, as you read His Word, ask God to convict you of anything that hinders His work in you.

Question 2: Is there a blessing I need to share?

Life is not about being selfish. Usually God will give you a promise, a thought, or an insight to share with someone you will meet during the day. Read with the assumption that He is equipping you to bless someone you meet during life's journey.

Question 3: What is the lesson I need to learn?

What is God trying to tell me about life? His Word is our manual for living. Often, while assembling toys for my children, I check the toy's manual for instructions and guidelines to ensure it will run correctly. As we read the Bible, we need to be ready for the lessons from the ultimate instruction manual.

Question 4: Is God showing me a trap I need to avoid?

When you discover something that God is saying to avoid, do not consider Him a "cosmic kill joy" but rather a loving, caring parent. He is helping you prevent a catastrophe! Think of it this way. When whitewater rafting through the rocky waters of Costa Rica, our guide gave us specific instructions about when to row, when to sit, and when to jump in the water. He lovingly told us not to dive in the water in dangerous areas. Was he trying to keep us from enjoying the adventure of the rapids? Just the opposite! He knew what areas of the stream could be deadly, and he warned us out of a desire for our best trip. God is your guide. He knows what areas are rocky and deadly, and he warns you out of love.

Question 5: What prayer needs to be prayed?

Throughout the Bible, we witness tremendous prayers of the faith. From the eloquence of Moses's prayer to the emotional intensity of Paul's prayer, we find perfect examples of how to be open and honest with God. Even in Psalms, as we read the prayers of David, we can grow closer to God's heart by imitating or even repeating His Words in our own prayers.

Now, you are equipped. You are ready to open God's Word and hear directly from Him today. For the next ten minutes, read the Bible and ask the Lord to speak directly to you. After reading a short passage, run through the five questions to personalize the ancient words to you. You will undoubtedly feel yourself emerge from the shadows with a greater ability to engage the world.

ENGAGING ENDEAVORS

Do you have a favorite book of the Bible? What do you like about it? Are there other books of the Bible that are similar? This might be a good place for you to start your Bible study.

What time of day is best for you to spend time in God's Word? Schedule time to study every day. Decide on a comfortable, quiet place in the house where you can focus. Place your Bible and journal in that room and get ready to listen to God speak. Make It a habit to study the Bible in that place, at that time each day.

DAILY TAKEAWAY

FROM TODAY'S DEVO -

WRITE SOMETHING DOWN.

_____

_____

_____

_____

_____

_____

PRAY SOMETHING THROUGH.

_____

_____

_____

_____

_____

PASS SOMETHING ALONG.

_____

_____

_____

_____

_____

Your Witness with The 42 Principle

"But when you pray, go into your room, close the door and pray to your Father, who is unseen. Then your Father, who sees what is done in secret, will reward you."

- Matthew 6:6

Would you believe that full-time ministry can make a person spiritually lazy? It's true! I can become so busy with God's work that I don't make time for my relationship with God.

I learned this when I lived in Pennsylvania and worked for the Billy Graham Crusade. It was both an honor and a challenge to work for a ministry that impacted so many people for Christ. It was easy for me to settle into that role and let my job be my relationship with Christ. One day, I had the chance to have lunch with an older pastor, Ben Smith, from a very large inner-city church. As we ate, I fired questions at him about church growth, corporate prayer, and excellence in ministry.

In the middle of my question-answer session, he basically called time-out, and he rocked my world by saying, "Scott, I am more concerned that God is happy with who I am than with what I do." The profoundness of this principle became a lifelong challenge to not let my work for the Lord become the basis of my relationship with Him.

One way to make sure you are putting your relationship with God over your work for Him is to remember the idea of DO versus DONE. In all other religions, your place in afterlife is based on what you DO during this lifetime. If you DO enough, you will have a positive afterlife. With Christ, our place in Heaven is not based on what we can DO, but on what He has DONE.

God certainly wants us to do good things in life, but those actions come after we have a personal relationship with Him. That relationship is why He created us in the first place! With a strong and healthy relationship with Christ, our good actions will come naturally.

With this idea in mind, we can go into the world and begin to make an impact.

2 Corinthians 5: 20 reads, "We are Christ's ambassadors, and God is using us to speak to you." Once God has spoken to you, He will use you to speak to others.

Think of where you spend your time. Where can you be an ambassador for Christ? Where can God speak to others through you? List the people you are in contact with in the following areas:

- Home with family–

- Work with partners–

- School with friends–

- Teams/Activities with people you closely work with–

- Church with those you worship with –

In all these relationships, God can speak through you, but your goal must be to please God in each area of life. Ask yourself, "Who am I trying to please? Who am I trying to impress at home, school, and church?" Are you trying to be liked, cool, or visible…even for Christ? Paul challenges us in Galatians 1:10 "Obviously, I'm not trying to be a people pleaser! No, I'm trying to please God. If I were still trying to please people, I would not be Christ's servant."

Several years after my lunch with Pastor Smith, I was meeting with the former President of the Billy Graham Association. He reminded me of my conversation with Pastor Smith by introducing me to The 42 Principle. It is, "Before I talk 4 God, I must talk 2 God." How many times do I get this backwards! So often, I talk to people on God's behalf before I have personally spoken to Him on a particular day. The challenge was restored to me that I must spend some time with him each day, letting God speak to me through His Word and speaking to Him through prayer before I talk to others about Him.

How can you make The 42 Principle real in your life? When you look at a building under construction, the foundation is typically simple and flat in appearance but the balance of the building relies on its foundation. Spending time with the Lord is similar. Time with Him does not have to be long and complicated, but it is foundational.

Charlie Riggs made this daily time easy to grasp with his 5/5/5 plan. For a quality time with the Lord, do the following...

> 5 Minutes – LISTEN. Read God's Word; learn His Will. The Bible is a love letter from God as well as His blueprint for our lives.

> 5 Minutes – TALK. Pray about everything! Prayer is more than "give me-s." It includes praise, thanksgiving, confession and sharing our innermost thoughts.

> 5 Minutes – PLAN. Set plans to do His work. As you worship, look for specific ways you can please God.

This simple 5/5/5 plan will help you talk 2 God before you talk 4 Him. It will root you in Him, as Paul described in Colossians. The spiritual fruits you want in your life and service for Him come from being rooted in Him. If you are just busy for Him, your life will be frustrated, empty and exhausted with activity. If you spend consistent time with Him, building your relationship with Him first, then you will become the kind of Christian who can change the world.

ENGAGING ENDEAVORS

Do you spend more time talking about God or talking to Him?

Do you spend more time praying out loud, in front of others, or praying alone?

How often do you pray for your friends before sharing with them?

 DAILY TAKEAWAY

FROM TODAY'S DEVO -

WRITE SOMETHING DOWN.

_____
_____
_____
_____
_____
_____

PRAY SOMETHING THROUGH.

_____
_____
_____
_____
_____

PASS SOMETHING ALONG.

_____
_____
_____
_____
_____

*"Through him all things were made; without him nothing
was made that has been made. In him was life, and that
life was the light of all mankind. The light shines in the
darkness, and the darkness has not overcome it."*

- John 1: 3-5

I was in a dark place in my life... literally. Every night I would shut the
door, turn off the lights, lie in bed, and listen to the radio. It was my
routine to listen to hip hop for thirty minutes and then switch to national
radio preachers on the Christian station. I had just moved to Florida
and the comforts of my previous neighborhood were gone. I had to say
goodbye to my friends, school, and ultimately, my Dad.

I was in a dark place spiritually, too. I didn't know Christ, and it felt like my
life was spiraling out of control. The partying, drinking, and arguing with
my parents were taking a toll. Plus, I felt alone in the crowd of my new
school. My insecurities rose to the surface each morning as I trudged off
to school and tried to make new friends again.

"If there really is a God, why is He allowing me to go through all this?" I
thought.

The answer to that question came from an unusual place. It began with
a conversation with a family member who challenged me to examine
my life. He asked me who came first in my life. At the time, I had never
thought about that. I mostly thought about music then. In fact, hip-hop
music dominated every aspect of my mind. It shaped how I viewed
myself, others, and even God.

My family member explained to me that God loved me, and that He wants
to have a relationship with me. He also told me that anything I put above
God was an idol, that God loved me too much to share me with anyone
or anything.

Those words hit home.

Later, as I flipped to the Christian station, I heard a pastor sharing the
Gospel. He explained that no matter where I was, I could give my life to
Christ and begin a new life. I dropped to my knees and prayed a simple

75

prayer. "God if you're really real, prove it to me, and I'll follow you the rest of my life." In that moment, I understood that I was lost. Ultimately, I was going to spend eternity separated from God because of the sin in my life. I cried out to God in the simplest way I could. I asked Him to save me.

ENGAGING ENDEAVORS

Find a room without windows and turn off the lights. Time yourself to see how long you can stand the darkness before you need to turn on a light.

Write down how you felt in the dark. What went through your mind? What made you finally emerge from the darkness?

Make a list of the people in your family who are "in the dark."

How can you tangibly reach out to them this week with the love of Christ?

DAILY TAKEAWAY

FROM TODAY'S DEVO -

WRITE SOMETHING DOWN.

_____

_____

_____

_____

_____

_____

PRAY SOMETHING THROUGH.

_____

_____

_____

_____

_____

PASS SOMETHING ALONG.

_____

_____

_____

_____

_____

"A father to the fatherless, a defender of widows, is God in his holy dwelling."

- Psalm 68:5

A father tells his son, "I promise I will take you fishing on Saturday." The little boy smiles with delight and begins planning the trip immediately. He begs Mom to take him to the store for fishing gear for this special weekend with Dad. This weekend, Dad will not just flip channels and fall asleep in the recliner. It's fishing time!

On Friday night, the little boy and his mother peruse the fishing section in Wal-Mart for plastic worms, lures, and a new hat. Mom pays for the items but wonders if her money is well spent. Her son might forget the many times Dad broke those promises, but she doesn't. She sighs and hopes for the best as they load the car and head home.

At home, the little boy races upstairs to reorganize his tackle box. He spends hours working on his fishing rods and then, just before turning off the lights, he lays out his clothes for the next morning. He falls asleep dreaming about the fun he will have with his dad.

That night, only a few hours later, his mother starts to cry. Her fear has turned to reality. The boy's father, notorious for going to the local bar on Friday night, is still out. Her rule of thumb is if he doesn't make it home by 10:00 PM, he probably would not come home at all. It's 11:30 PM and she sees no sign of his dad. She feels tears rolling down her cheek as she wonders what to say to her son the next morning.

Mom cries herself to sleep.

The next morning, her son wakes her up at 5:00 AM. "Wake up, Mom! I have to get ready. Dad and I are going fishing soon!" The little boy looks around. All the lights in the house are off. Dad's car is not parked outside. He is not making coffee. The house is silent. The little boy looks at his mom, and her eyes tell the rest of the story. She hugs him, and they cry themselves back to sleep.

The little boy in this story is me. I grew up with an alcoholic father who took his own life when I was seventeen years old. I accepted Christ when I was eighteen.

I never got a chance to tell my father about the greatest thing that had ever happened to me. He did not see my baptism. He never heard the first Bible study I taught, or the first sermon I preached. He never got to know my beautiful wife or his amazing grandchildren. He never got to see me share Christ with people across the globe or speak at international universities or defend the Gospel to Muslims.

I have had the opportunity to share Christ with so many people, including my father's old drinking buddies, but I never had the opportunity to share with my dad. If only he'd lived another year! I feel so much sorrow that my dad never knew God.

And yet, I see people who could walk down the hall and share with their dad, but they don't. I see friends who could pick up a phone and tell their dad about Jesus, but they don't. I would do anything to have one more day or one more hour with my dad to share the good news of the Gospel, but I can't.

Maybe you think your parents don't want to hear it, but trust me, the pain of their rejection is nothing compared with the sadness of allowing them to die without knowing the Savior. Don't wait until it's too late. If you still have the opportunity to share with your mom and dad, go for it. You will never regret the decision to share about the Perfect Parent with your parent.

ENGAGING ENDEAVORS

What fears do you have about sharing the Gospel and your faith with your dad? What fears do you have about sharing with your mom?

What do you think he/she would say or do if you just shared your testimony today?

Can you commit to pray for your mom and dad regularly? If they already know Christ, then you can pray for their faith to be strengthened and for God to use them mightily. If they do not know Christ, be faithful in prayer and obedient to God's leading for you to share.

DAILY TAKEAWAY

FROM TODAY'S DEVO -

WRITE SOMETHING DOWN.

_____
_____
_____
_____
_____
_____

PRAY SOMETHING THROUGH.

_____
_____
_____
_____
_____

PASS SOMETHING ALONG.

_____
_____
_____
_____
_____
_____

Your Siblings with Love

"If anyone says, 'I love God,' and hates his brother, he is a liar; for he who does not love his brother whom he has seen cannot love God whom he has not seen."

- 1 John 4:20

How many pranks have you played on your brother or sister? How many times have you inflicted physical pain or emotional embarrassment on them? I must admit I have done the following:

- Rubbed Icy Hot in my brother's eye
- Burned him with an iron
- Chipped his tooth on the tile floor
- Punched him in the face
- Locked him in many closets

And that's just the tip of the iceberg! I can honestly say that I abused my poor little brother until he was fifteen years old. That is the year he grew five inches and twenty pounds, and he got revenge for all the years of torture.

And yet, if anyone I knew spoke a negative word about him, I would not allow it. If my friends tried to hurt him, I stopped them. If I saw him in trouble, I did not hesitate to come to his rescue.

If you have siblings, you understand. YOU are allowed to abuse them, but no one else.

Why is this? I think it's because, deep down, we have a profound love for our brothers and sisters. Although they annoy us to no end when we are young, the truth is, we love 'em.

One of the most memorable moments of my wedding occurred at the rehearsal dinner. My brother stood up to begin the toasts, and he described me as, "perfect." After all we'd been through together, after all the wedgies, noogies, punch bugs, and pranks, he saw the best in me, and I will never forget it.

How would you describe your siblings? If you are young, you might still see some annoying qualities in them, but look past the daily irritations and think about what you see. Do you see someone who knows God? Do you see a Christian? Do you see a girl who is struggling to find her place in the world? Do you see a little boy who wants to be accepted?

You might be the only one who knows the truth about your sibling. You hear them crying in their room after a breakup. You know when they argue with your parents. You are there when they wake up in the morning and when they throw their book bag on the kitchen table as they come home from school.

That means you have a great opportunity! You can minister to your brothers and sisters in their time of need. You can introduce them to Jesus, if they don't know Him. You have more time with them than almost anyone. Even if you lead busy lives, you are still forced to see them more often than almost anyone on the planet.

Hebrews 13:1 reads, "Keep on loving each other as brothers." This verse assumes that you actually LOVE your brother. What better way to love your brother than to pray for them, instruct them in truth, and point them to Christ?

If you and your siblings have a good relationship, you may even have the opportunity to sharpen one another. Proverbs 27:17 tells us, "As iron sharpens iron, so one man sharpens another." Why waste time with your siblings just watching television, playing video games, or fighting over the bathroom? Below are four ideas for ways you could take the lead in creating a relationship that glorifies God and encourages your siblings.

Prayer List – Hang a dry erase board in your room and ask your siblings how you can pray for them each week. Then, be sure to let them know that you have prayed for their request. You can also display your prayer requests and hope that they will join you.

Sibling Bible Study – If you are studying a certain book, invite your brother or sister to read with you. Informally discuss what God is teaching you on a regular basis so your conversations can be full of grace.

Serve Together – Take the lead to find a place where you can help people in your neighborhood or community. Plan the service event in advance so your siblings can mark their calendar and join you.

Accountability Questions – If your brother or sister is spiritually strong, they could make a great accountability partner! Discuss what you are learning in this book and ask them to hold you accountable for following through with your decisions during these thirty days.

ENGAGING ENDEAVORS

Have your siblings accepted Christ? If not, take time to pray for their salvation and for opportunities to share with them.

If you had to guess, what are your brothers and sisters struggling with right now? Pray for God to lead them through these struggles and use you to minister to them.

DAILY TAKEAWAY

FROM TODAY'S DEVO -

WRITE SOMETHING DOWN.

_____
_____
_____
_____
_____
_____

PRAY SOMETHING THROUGH.

_____
_____
_____
_____
_____
_____

PASS SOMETHING ALONG.

_____
_____
_____
_____
_____
_____

A Friend with Hope

"May the God of hope fill you with all joy and peace in believing, so that by the power of the Holy Spirit you may abound in hope."

- Romans 15:13

Now that you are a follower of Christ, how do you relate to your friends who knew you before you surrendered your life? You may think, "I don't have the courage to talk to them about God because they will not take me seriously."

I'm here to tell you that you are wrong. If your friends could tell you how they feel, they would reveal a world of hurt, confusion, and insecurity. Believe me, your friends spend more time covering up their real identity than you suspect.

Not only are your friends insecure, they are also blinded to the truth that they are so desperate to see. 2 Corinthians 4:4 tells us that the enemy of this age blinds the eyes of unbelievers. Your friends may think they need more athletic ability, beauty, or intelligence to ease their adolescent pain, but we know that they need Christ. Read the example below about four men who brought their friend to Christ.

Jesus stepped into a boat, crossed over and came to his own town. Some men brought to him a paralytic, lying on a mat. When Jesus saw their faith, he said to the paralytic, "Take heart, son; your sins are forgiven." At this, some of the teachers of the law said to themselves, "This fellow is blaspheming!" Knowing their thoughts, Jesus said, "Why do you entertain evil thoughts in your hearts? Which is easier: to say, 'Your sins are forgiven,' or to say, 'Get up and walk'? But so that you may know that the Son of Man has authority on earth to forgive sins...." Then he said to the paralytic, "Get up, take your mat and go home." And the man got up and went home. When the crowd saw this, they were filled with awe; and they praised God, who had given such authority to men. (Mark 2:1-12)

Imagine the life of the paralyzed man in this story. He lives his life on a mat. He can't go anywhere or do anything without the help of loved ones. Many of your friends are living life on a mat, too. They may not be physically paralyzed, but they are stuck in some form or another. They could be paralyzed by fear, worry, guilt, shame, uncertainty, or some other personal struggle.

But, thankfully, the paralytic in this story had people in his life who loved him enough to bring him to Jesus. And Jesus not only healed his physical pain, but he also healed his deepest spiritual need, his need for forgiveness. Jesus did not disappoint the paralytic, and he will not disappoint your friends.

So what is Jesus looking for when he sees us trying to help a friend? Did Jesus say, "Look at how strong these guys are to have carried him all this way?" No. Did he say, "Look at how many came to help just one person?" No. Did he say, look at their determination and fortitude?" No. Jesus said, "Look at their faith!"

Jesus is waiting for you to step out on faith and bring your friends to Him. It takes faith to take a step. Don't worry if you do not know exactly what to say or what to do. God will lead your heart as you step out for your friends. The soles of your shoes must follow where the soul of your life leads.

Because you have been reconciled to God through Christ, you are called to do the work of reconciliation for others. Your goal is to reflect what you have received. This is your ministry! This is where the Christian life gets fun – and a little messy. But you are commanded to do it. So, be strong and courageous. Be the best friend anyone can have. Pick up the mats of your friends and walk them to Jesus.

ENGAGING ENDEAVORS

What fears grip you when you think about engaging your friends with the Gospel?

Would you stop and pray right now that God would take those fears away and that he would open up moments and different times where it is obvious he wants you to talk about Jesus?

Take a second and write down the first person you know is down on their mat and paralyzed unless Jesus steps in. Now write down some names of believing friends that would help you carry your friend and their mat to Jesus. One person on their mat: _____

My friends of faith who will help carry this person: _____

_____

DAILY TAKEAWAY

FROM TODAY'S DEVO -

WRITE SOMETHING DOWN.

_____

_____

_____

_____

_____

_____

PRAY SOMETHING THROUGH.

_____

_____

_____

_____

_____

PASS SOMETHING ALONG.

_____

_____

_____

_____

_____

_____

Your School
with Prayer

"Pray without ceasing."

- 1 Thessalonians 5:17

Have you ever been part of a team? Have you played a sport, marched in the band, or competed with a group of people to win a prize? If so, I am sure you had a game plan for winning and you practiced that plan often.

Today, you will be developing a plan for a much bigger game.

Here is the game. Your task is to win as many unbelieving students in your school to Christ as possible before you leave for college. So, if you were approaching this like a sport or school challenge, what would you do? You'd create a plan and work on it everyday, just like you practice almost everyday for your sport.

Most students, however, only study the playbook once per week, at church. Would you ever join a team with the expectation that you'll only practice once per week? Probably not. With this strategy, your team won't win much.

So, what is your strategy? I suggest starting with your school. Almost every American teenager is funneled through the public or private school system in this country, so your campus is one of the greatest mission fields in your community. In fact, campuses across this nation are one of the richest mission fields available.

As a student, you are forced to emerge from your home daily with hundreds of other students and activities going on at your school. Most adults don't have such interaction on a regular basis. You are in the middle of the game more often than many Christian leaders, preachers, and evangelists. This means that you have an opportunity to engage in a way that even I can't.

I am not pretending that it's easy to engage your school, but with God, all things are possible. The first question to ask yourself is, "Do I have a desire to see my school changed for the glory of God?" If so, heed the words of 2 Chronicles 7:14. "If my people, who are called by my name, will humble themselves and pray and seek my face and turn from their wicked ways, then will I hear from heaven and will forgive their sin and will heal their land."

The second question to ask yourself is, "Am I willing to pray for my student body?"

Prayer is an activity we love to talk about as Christians but rarely do. Prayer is your greatest weapon against the enemy's work in your school. Don't be afraid to pray big prayers, those that are destined to fail unless God steps in.

Students all over the country are becoming prayer warriors. It's exciting! I see prayer requests on Facebook and Twitter, and I see teenagers drowning their schools in prayer.

One of the most creative ideas I've seen is called, "Project Locker Combination." If you'd like to try it, you will need a prepaid phone that can receive text messages. I would suggest getting your youth pastor and principal on board so it will be successful. Simply drop a note in every locker at your school that reads, "If you are hurting or needing prayer for something, text your prayer requests to this number xxx-xxxx. If you send a prayer request, you don't have to give us your name, but please give us your locker number so we can drop a note in there letting you know we prayed for you."

I know a school that did this, and it was immediately successful. They received as many as thirty texts per day. If Project Locker Combination sounds like something you'd like to try, here are a few helpful hints:

- Assemble a team of students who are committed to praying.

- Enroll the help of leaders through organizations like First Priority, Young Life, or your local church.

- Assign one student to be in charge of the phone each week.

- Keep the phone in silent mode so you don't disrupt class.

- Check with your local church to see if they will pay for the monthly cell phone bill.

If your school does not allow phones, then I highly recommend an alternate idea called the 333 Project. Go to 333project.com to check out how to implement it in your community. It's based on Jeremiah 33:3, which says, "Call to me and I will answer you and tell you great and unsearchable things you do not know." All you have to do is set your cell phone alarm to go off at 3:33 PM everyday. When you hear the alarm, you are reminded to pray for your principal, administration, teacher, students, and church.

Project Locker Combination and Project 333 are two examples of game plans to glorify God at your school. You can implement these projects or think of your own, but don't miss out on the opportunity you have as a student. Pray for other students. Engage your mission field. Be a part of the revolution!

ENGAGING ENDEAVORS

Stop right now and ask God to break your heart for the lost students at your school. Ask him to give you the courage to engage in prayer for them.

Decide if you want to begin a prayer project at your school. Take some time to brainstorm ideas for leading others to pray at your school.

Set up a time to talk to your youth pastor to get their leadership helping you. Remember, there are no lone rangers in the Kingdom of God!

DAILY TAKEAWAY

FROM TODAY'S DEVO -

WRITE SOMETHING DOWN.

_____

_____

_____

_____

_____

PRAY SOMETHING THROUGH.

_____

_____

_____

_____

PASS SOMETHING ALONG.

_____

_____

_____

_____

_____

enGaGe:

Social Media and
The Virtual World

"We are therefore Christ's ambassadors, as though God were making his appeal through us. We implore you on Christ's behalf: Be reconciled to God."

- 2 Corinthians 5:20

What if you had a microphone to the world? If you had five minutes to convey one important message to thousands of people, what would you say? You have a tool that will allow you to speak to the world. Today, we will focus on having an influence in the virtual world. This includes Facebook, Twitter, YouTube, blogs, websites, and more.

The first step to making a difference online is to realize that you are a witness, everywhere, including on the internet. Everything you type online counts. Think of LeBron James. He is a spokesperson for everything from cell phones to tennis shoes. When he Tweets about shoes, people buy them. When he updates his status that he is eating at a particular restaurant, his fans want to eat there, too. He endorses products and places he likes.

So, what are you endorsing? Who are you endorsing? Do you have a permanent endorsement contract with Jesus?

Your words do not have to scream, "Jesus is my man!" Every time you post a picture, video, or status update, you reveal what you really believe. You may have heard the adage, "A picture is worth a thousand words." And now, that picture has a permanent link to your name. Jesus tells us in Mark, "Their lips praise me, but their hearts are far away from me." It's important to live a life of such integrity that our words, pictures, and updates portray the same message.

One year, at a youth conference, we interviewed people on the street about Jesus. One young lady had been drinking on Friday night and she was way too drunk to say anything coherent. She signed the waiver, agreeing to let us use her footage, and proceeded to embarrass herself. The video was shown on Sunday morning, and guess who was in the congregation? The young lady from the video! True story!

Could you imagine her shock when the entire church saw her inebriated state? Scripture says whatever is done in private will be brought out in public. This is so true online. Do not do ANYTHING without the understanding that it can be captured and shown to the entire universe.

However, making an impact online is more than just keeping your image squeaky clean.

Have you ever considered doing something creative online? Start a Facebook discussion about your faith. We have an excellent resource called sharingthefaith.com, which teaches you how to share your faith. It is possible for you to go online, develop your testimony, and then be able to share your testimony to everyone on your contact list!

When developing your testimony, consider four stages of your life. First, describe your life before Christ. Second, describe how you came to know Christ. Third, tell how Christ came into your life and fourth, let people know what God is doing in your life now. You never know who needs to hear your before and after story. Someone is still living in the BEFORE part of their story. Your testimony could lead them closer to the AFTER part.

Another way to start an online revolution is to start a prayer chain. Create a focus group where people can ask for prayer and be prayed for on a daily basis.

Finally, consider creating a virtual crusade. Start small with a group of friends that can share their faith. Target friends who are without Christ with the intent of sharing Christ. Start with friendly discussion. Share common interests and then, open the discussion to thoughts about God and religion. Then, when the time is right, share your story. Share what Christ has done for you and ask if this has happened to them.

Begin with a prayer like this....

"Dear Father. You know me. I want every part of my life to be used for your glory. Sometimes, my own pursuits distract me, and I ask your forgiveness. Today, I ask that you use me to encourage others and point to you. Allow me to use this online tool for your glory. Protect me from the evil one, and make me a witness for you in the real world as well as the virtual world. Thank you for this opportunity to make an impact for eternity."

What can you do to make sure your values shine through on Facebook, Twitter, and YouTube?

Do you have any creative ideas for sharing your faith online?

DAILY TAKEAWAY

FROM TODAY'S DEVO -

WRITE SOMETHING DOWN.

_____

_____

_____

_____

_____

PRAY SOMETHING THROUGH.

_____

_____

_____

_____

_____

PASS SOMETHING ALONG.

_____

_____

_____

_____

_____

Truth by
Battling Relativism

"Teach me Your way, O Lord, that I may walk and live in Your truth; direct and unite my heart to fear and honor Your name."

- Psalm 86:11

In a national survey, 83% of teenagers said truth depends on circumstances while only 6% said truth is absolute. So, many young people in this country would say that truth is relative. This philosophy is called Relativism.

Relativism is the position that every person's point of view is equally valid. It asserts that all truth is based on individual feelings about a particular subject. So, if someone is sincere about what they believe, relativists do not worry that they are sincerely wrong.

Because relativism runs rampant, many sins that were once considered wrong are not only accepted but are even promoted in our society. As a Christian, we are making a bold statement to assert that there is one God, that there is one Way, that there is one Truth. This idea is wildly countercultural. It takes guts to stand up to the thunder of relativism that shouts, "Nothing is wrong! You can do whatever feels right to you! If you believe it's right, it probably is!"

Relative truths do have a place in our society, though. For example, when a person says, "Blue is better than green," they are asserting an opinion, or a truth that only applies to them. This person will be more likely to buy blue clothes or drive a blue car. But not everything is relative. For example, seven is always greater than five. Unfortunately, our society has become so confused, they basically believe that seven might be greater than five, if you believe it is.

This thought pattern has translated to thoughts about the Bible. People believe, "The Bible may be true for you, but it's not true for me." But the Bible does not belong in the colors category. It belongs in the math category. It is always true. Its words are always right. It is truth.

But isn't the Bible like the other holy books, like the Quran or the Book of Mormon? In a word, no. The Bible is unlike any holy book on the planet.

The Quran was written by one author, Mohammed, over a span of a few years. The Book of Mormon was written by one man, Joseph Smith, over a span of ten years. But the Bible was written by more than forty authors, spanning sixteen hundred years, and yet it fits together like pieces of a puzzle. Although the authors did not know each other, the theme of the Bible is consistent and staggeringly coherent.

In addition, there are over 24,000 partial and complete manuscript copies of the New Testament available today. From a historical point of view, this makes the Bible one of the most reliable documents in history.

If you are looking for more than just historical authenticity, check out the over three hundred promises given to Old Testament prophets that have been fulfilled. These promises were not just guesses; they were all pointing to one Messiah. They were telling of an anointed Savior coming to the world for the single purpose of saving people from their sins. The probability of one man accidentally fulfilling all those promises is 1 in 1 with 157 zeros behind it. You would have a better chance of dropping a cork in the ocean, waiting a year, and then trying to find it, then having a single man make all those prophesies come true.

Isaiah 40:8 reads, "The grass withers and the flowers fade, but the word of our God stands forever." It's time to emerge from the idea that all ideas are the same. God's Word is truth. It is wise to place your faith on a book that been proven authentic by every standard.

Emerge from relativism and stand on truth.

ENGAGING ENDEAVORS

Read Psalm 86:11 again and make it your prayer today.

Pray that God will give you the answers to defend your stance for truth with gentleness and discretion.

When you are confused by verses in the Bible, contact your pastor directly. I promise he will be thrilled to share what God has revealed about His Word.

DAILY TAKEAWAY

FROM TODAY'S DEVO -

WRITE SOMETHING DOWN.

_____
_____
_____
_____
_____
_____

PRAY SOMETHING THROUGH.

_____
_____
_____
_____
_____

PASS SOMETHING ALONG.

_____
_____
_____
_____
_____

DAY 11 *engage:*

Heaven with
The 146 Engagement

"I and the Father are one."

– John 10:30

What would happen if you phoned a restaurant and asked, "Can I speak to the President of the United States?" What would be the response? "Uh, I'm sorry. He's not here. Try the White House!" If you want to talk to the President, you need to know his phone number.

In the same way, we cannot dial any random number and hope to speak with God. You need to know His direct line. All numbers do not lead to the same place, and all religions do not lead to God.

Jesus said these words about the direct number to God. I like to call it, The 146 Engagement. In John 14:6, Jesus said, "I am the way and the truth and the life. No one comes to the Father except through me." Of all the statements uttered by Jesus, none outrages our culture like this one. What He is saying is that if you want to engage God in an eternal way, then you must go through His Son.

We think it's great that God became flesh and dwelt among us. But when we consider Jesus' claim to be the only way, we might feel uncomfortable. Isn't this narrow-minded? Is it intolerant? Are Christians building an elite country club that excludes everyone who does not think the same way they do? These are common questions our culture asks, so we need to be ready with an answer.

It's simple. Since the Garden of Eden, there has been a gap between man and God. Our sin separates us from the perfection of God, and sin demands payment. Jesus made the payment by living a sinless life and dying on the cross for everything we have done wrong in the past, present, and future. He offers every person on earth the chance to accept the gift of eternal life. Anyone can get off their selfish path and engage the 146 Life.

Although none of us deserve the 146 Life, we all have an opportunity to accept it. It's a freeway that Christ paved for us to reach God. And He did

103

this for us while we were sinners. This is what separates Christianity from all world religions. God is not asking us to earn our way into heaven. He is not requiring anything other than our willingness to hop on the road He provided.

Other religions subscribe to a Home Depot Philosophy for getting to heaven. Home Depot's slogan is "You can do it. We can help." If you buy into Home Depot's philosophy, you want to do-it-yourself. You want a religion where you work hard and hope for the best. Other religions tell you, "You can do it. Build your own freeway to God." If you buy into this idea, you are always trying to be strong enough, right enough, and perfect enough.

No matter how hard you work, you cannot build your own path to God.

Luckily, you don't have to. The freeway is finished. Christ built it. So, as much as we'd like to think, "Buddhism, Hinduism, and Christianity are basically the same," they are not. In Christianity, the road is complete. In other religions, you have to build it.

The question I often hear is, "But what about my friend who sincerely believes in a philosophy other than Christianity?" My answer is that they are sincerely wrong. However, there is good news for that person who is sincerely seeking God. Jeremiah 29:13 reads, "You will find me when you seek me with all your heart." And Jesus is looking for these people. He tells us that He came to seek and save the lost. So, Jesus is looking for people who are looking for Him.

In other words, the Holy Spirit affords us the opportunity to seek God. He is working out the whole deal. If we are truly seeking God, what's going to happen? God will reveal himself to you, to your friends, and to your family. If you are sitting here right now as a follower of Jesus Christ, I want to encourage you to take the 146 Engagement and apply it to your faith, your family, your friends, and your future.

Don't let the confusion of our culture trick you into believing that truth is a lie and a lie is truth. Engage your world with Jesus. He is the only direct number to God.

ENGAGING ENDEAVORS

Read Matthew 7:13-14. Take a good look at your heart. Would you honestly say that you are on the 146 Highway even though it is a narrow road and few ever find it? If your answer is yes, take a second and thank God for revealing himself to you!

Think of one family member or friend you know who might subscribe to the Home Depot philosophy of heaven. They believe they can build the road themselves. They believe God is going to give them a pass because they are a good person. Would you pray that John 14:6 would come out of your mouth and impact their life forever?

 DAILY TAKEAWAY

FROM TODAY'S DEVO -

WRITE SOMETHING DOWN.

PRAY SOMETHING THROUGH.

PASS SOMETHING ALONG.

God's Past through the Old Testament

"These commandments that I give you today are to be on your hearts."

- Deuteronomy 6:6

As a pastor, I often hear questions about the end times and the book of Revelation. Although it's natural to wonder about our future, it would be more beneficial to study the past, to learn how we've arrived at this juncture in history, and what God has taught His people for thousands of years.

It's true that students study American history, European history, and even the history of western civilization, but rarely do our history books go back far enough to see the whole picture. The Old Testament is the place to discover God's handiwork and to see a foreshadowing of His later work.

I believe our ignorance about the past is one of Satan's great victories. If he can cause us to forget what God has done, then he keeps us from being equipped for today. An understanding of the Old Testament will even help us understand current events. I recently studied Daniel with a group of college students and they were amazed by how relevant the information was to present-day world news. For example, we often hear about the animosity between Palestinians and Israelites on television. But do we know what the Old Testament says about these feuding groups?

In Daniel, Chapter 2, King Nebuchadnezzar had a dream. The dream bewildered him so much that he called for magicians, sorcerers, and enchanters to interpret it, but no one was able to tell him what the dream meant. Read what Daniel says.

Your Majesty looked, and there before you stood a large statue—an enormous, dazzling statue, awesome in appearance. The head of the statue was made of pure gold, its chest and arms of silver, its belly and thighs of bronze, its legs of iron, its feet partly of iron and partly of baked clay. While you were watching, a rock was cut out, but not by human hands. It struck the statue on its feet of iron and clay and smashed them. Then the iron, the clay, the bronze, the silver and the gold were all broken to pieces and became like chaff on a threshing floor in the summer. The wind swept them away without leaving a trace. But the rock that struck the statue became a huge mountain and filled the whole earth. (Daniel 2:31-35)

What on earth does that mean and how could it possibly relate to us? First, let's have a quick lesson of the symbols in the dream:

GOLD HEAD – King Nebuchadnezzar's Kingdom was likened to gold because it was an absolute monarchy.

SILVER CHEST – Represents the Medo-Persian Empire who would conquer Persia next

BRONZE BELLY – Represents the Greeks, led by Alexander the Great, who took over next

IRON LEGS – Represent the Roman Empire, which splits into the Western and Eastern Empire.

FEET OF IRON and CLAY – Represents how the Roman Empire will be split and made up of weak and strong nations.

The Bible predicts that the Roman Empire will never be united again. We know that many leaders throughout history have unsuccessfully tried to unite the Roman Empire. Charlemagne, Otto the great, Charles IV, Louis XIV, Napoleon, Bismarck, the Ottomans, and Adolph Hitler all tried ... and failed! And even now, the Israelites and Palestinians quarrel without resolution.

The final prediction in King Nebuchadnezzar's dream is that a rock will shatter the whole statue. Guess who the "Rock" is? You've got it! Jesus Christ.

Jesus is the Rock and the Chief Cornerstone according to Acts 4: 11 and Ephesians 2: 20. That is why Daniel said in 2:44, "In the days of those kings, the God of heaven will set up a kingdom which will never be destroyed, and that kingdom will not be left for another people; it will crush and put an end to all these kingdoms, but it will itself endure forever."
So, why did I just take you on a bullet train through history? First, it's amazing to realize that God predicted these events hundreds of years before they occurred. Second, it's important that we realize that Jesus is not just a person who lived for thirty-three years. History hinges on his life, resurrection, and coming again.

Engage God's past so you can have a complete understanding of what He is doing today and what is coming in the future.

ENGAGING ENDEAVORS

Revelation 11:15 reads, "The kingdom of the world has become the kingdom of our Lord and of his Christ, and he will reign for ever and ever." How is this verse different to you now that you know the history of King Nebuchadnezzar's dream?

What small steps can you take to engage God's past through the Old Testament? What has hindered you from reading this in the past?

Read Proverbs 22:28. What do you think this verse is saying to your generation about the Bible?

DAILY TAKEAWAY

FROM TODAY'S DEVO -

WRITE SOMETHING DOWN.

_____
_____
_____
_____
_____

PRAY SOMETHING THROUGH.

_____
_____
_____
_____
_____

PASS SOMETHING ALONG.

_____
_____
_____
_____
_____

"No one knows about that day or hour, not even the angels in heaven, nor the Son, but only the Father. Two men will be in the field; one will be taken and the other left. Two women will be grinding with the hand mill; one will be taken and the other left. Therefore keep watch, because you do not know on what day your Lord will come."

- Matthew 24:36,40, 42

Life is ironic, isn't it? You spend your young days wishing life would hurry up, and your latter days praying it would slow down. I remember, as a kid, I could not wait until I was big enough to sit in a big boy seat rather than a booster seat. Then, as I got older, I couldn't wait to enter high school, have a locker, drive a car, go on a date, start college, finish college, get a job, find a spouse, have a baby... Then, I couldn't wait for my children to talk, walk, go to school, graduate, and move out.

Now that I've witnessed all those things I wished for, I look back and it's all a blur. I understand the truth in James 4:14. "Why, you do not even know what will happen tomorrow. What is your life? You are a mist that appears for a little while and then vanishes."

Did you know that God created time? God is not bound by time, but mankind has been bound by time since the Garden of Eden. In Genesis 3:19, we read, "By the sweat of your brow you will eat your food until you return to the ground, since from it you were taken; for dust you are and to dust you will return."

From this point forward, mankind was put on a timetable and given a certain number of days on earth. Hebrews 9:27 says we all have an appointment with death, and we do not have the privilege of knowing when that appointment is coming. Because of the curse in Genesis 3, time is being lost year after year, month after month, day after day, and minute after minute.

So, we are all counting the days until our death, whether we realize it or not. Although no one likes to think about it, time is ticking. Life is short. And our lives here determine our eternity.

If our days are numbered and our time here is short, we must carefully choose how to live each day. I used to believe that my life should point to the Cross everyday, but now, I know that the Old Testament, New Testament, and all of Creation points to something even greater than the Cross. It points to the resurrection and the return of Christ.

1 Thessalonians 4:13-14 reads, "And now, brothers and sisters, I want you to know what will happen to the Christians who have died so you will not be full of sorrow like people who have no hope. For since we believe that Jesus died and was raised to life again, we also believe that when Jesus comes, God will bring back with Jesus all the Christians who have died."

There are three truths we all must swallow. First, we will die. Second, we don't know when. Third, Jesus is returning to bring us to heaven with Him.

The typical response to such sad news is to avoid thinking about it. It's easy to allow our subconscious mind to tell us, "Life is long! You are only in high school. You have years and years to figure out how to live for Christ. You don't have to fully surrender today."

But Scripture does not promise a long life. In fact, it's just the opposite. The Bible says you are not promised tomorrow. Our community was reminded of this fact when a beloved student was driving only a few minutes from her house when she lost control of her car and ran into a tree. Just like that, her beautiful life was taken from this earth. And she had it all! She was a cheerleader; she was loved by her community; she had hundreds of friends. But she was not promised tomorrow and neither are you.

Martin Luther, one of the most influential Christian leaders who ever lived, understood how short life is. He knew that God did not promise him college, marriage, children, grandchildren, and retirement. God has only promised to return and take us with him. Martin Luther said, "Prepare me Lord today for that day. Help me to live this day as if it was that day."

ENGAGING ENDEAVORS

1. Read James 4:13-17. What are these scriptures saying to you about your future and how you should live?

2. Stop and pray. Ask yourself, if I died tomorrow, what would I leave undone?

3. Challenge: Make a to-do list out of the items you wrote in question two. Then, spend however long it takes completing that task list. Do everything on the list before that day arrives.

DAILY TAKEAWAY

FROM TODAY'S DEVO -

WRITE SOMETHING DOWN.

_____

_____

_____

_____

_____

PRAY SOMETHING THROUGH.

_____

_____

_____

_____

_____

PASS SOMETHING ALONG.

_____

_____

_____

_____

_____

Ultimate
Responsibility

"For as the body apart from the spirit is dead, so also faith apart from works is dead."

- James 2:26

Do you ever watch the political debates? It's so depressing. All the candidates point fingers and blame others for the problems in our country. For once, wouldn't it be refreshing for someone to say, "It is my fault. It is your fault. It is our fault." We all need to take responsibility for the current state of the Union.

One preacher in England had the guts to take such a stance. The Times of London published an article pressing people to find who was at fault for the social ills of their time. C.K. Chesterton responded with one word, "Mine."

C.K. Chesterton took responsibility for his country. Who else will join him?

There is great risk in taking responsibility. You must count the cost for taking on the pain of the world. It is not for the faint of heart. It will take tenacity and focus. Jesus talks about counting the cost before going into war. No one flippantly engages in battle without seriously considering what's at stake.

On the other hand, there is great reward in taking responsibility. The world does not take time to celebrate people who strive for mediocrity. Only those who take charge will be remembered. When studying history, I am always amazed by the big difference individual people can make. Groups do not change history. Individuals who lead and inspire groups change it. Moses, David, Joseph, Paul, Martin Luther, and Billy Graham are a few of the ones God used to change the course of history. Of course, it always takes a team, but it is the individual who rises up to take responsibility who will be the one God chooses to work through.

When I was facing some difficult challenges in ministry, I decided to step off the stage and take on the role of facilitator. I did not want the challenges of responsibility, but I was torn because I knew God had given me a dream of taking students into cities to share their faith. I tried to convince other preachers to take the lead, but one night, my dear friend, Josh McDowell spoke wisdom into my life.

Josh told me, "God always uses people to carry out His will. Either be the man God desires, or step out of the way because He wants to use you to do great things." WOW! I was being told that if I wanted to be used then the cost was responsibility, but if I was going to step aside, God will do His work. I decided to take responsibility, and God blessed it. We trained tens of thousands of students and led our largest outreach event to date.

When you look at your life, it must revolve around taking responsibility. You are not responsible for where you have been placed in life - that is God's sovereignty, but you are responsible for where you are heading in life. Life is not a video game with multiple lives. You only have one shot at it. Make life count!

Take small steps today toward taking greater responsibility. Read a new book. Discover a new fact. Turn off the television and study your Bible. You cannot keep doing the same things over and over again expecting different results.

Finally, today do something that makes life better for someone else. This is the first step toward taking greater responsibility. Live as if what you do today matters for eternity. Why? Because it does.

ENGAGING ENDEAVORS

Do you feel a burden for something wrong in our country that you want to take responsibility for? Do you see something wrong in your area that you could lead the charge to change?

Take time to pray that God will show you how to lead the charge to change.

Even though you are willing to lead, the ultimate leader is Christ. By submitting to His will, you are becoming a servant leader. Look for areas in your school, town, state, country, and world to lead as God leads you.

DAILY TAKEAWAY

FROM TODAY'S DEVO -

WRITE SOMETHING DOWN.

_____
_____
_____
_____
_____
_____

PRAY SOMETHING THROUGH.

_____
_____
_____
_____
_____
_____

PASS SOMETHING ALONG.

_____
_____
_____
_____
_____
_____

"Therefore go and make disciples of all nations, baptizing them in the name of the Father and of the Son and of the Holy Spirit."

- Matthew 28:19

Congratulations! You have walked through the shadows and emerged to a new place in your life. You have already begun to make an impact, and now it's time to spend the rest of your days changing the world.

If you are thinking, "Who am I to change the world?" That's okay. If you feel inadequate, that's okay, too. Every spiritual giant recognizes his or her personal inadequacy. Remember the disciples. They were not the best and brightest. They did not have a business plan or Excel spreadsheet outlining the best way to change the world, but God used them, and He will use you.

Remember, it's not what YOU can do, but what GOD can do through you.

In Acts 1:8, Jesus tells us that we are His witnesses, and our mission field is Jerusalem, Judea, Samaria, and the ends of the earth. I used to think this was purely a geographic strategy. While it is such a strategy, it is also much more. It is a racial strategy. Samaria was another race. It's also about your comfort zone, starting with people you are most comfortable with and moving outward. It's about God's plan. It's His strategy for making an impact. He told the disciples how to reach out.

So it is now with us in America in the twenty-first century. Where are our sights? What is your vision to see change happen? Where is your Jerusalem? Is it your family? Is it your best friend? Your Jerusalem includes the people closest to you. You cannot go on a mission trip to share Jesus and not share Him with your parents and neighbors.

Your Judea includes your surroundings. Think of people you have contact with regularly. This includes co-workers, classmates, or even distant friends you see occasionally. Pray first and foremost. God has workers in the field to be used to see people come to know Christ. Remember the words of Paul. "Some plant and some water, but He is the Lord of the harvest." Pray that God will bring light into their life and grow the seeds you sprinkle.

Samaria is different for all of us. It is out of our comfort zone. It could be working with children in your community who don't have strong role models. It could mean volunteering at a homeless shelter. It could even be intentionally developing friendships that are about sharing Christ. Take this as an opportunity to grow in life experience.

We must be careful not to skip over the other parts of the plan to go to the ends of the earth. It will not be a good witness to people in your community if you are serving people in other countries while ignoring needs in your backyard. You must do what the Lord has placed in your heart, but a balanced approach is what we see in the book of Acts.

How can you start a movement? Be sensitive to God's spirit. He is looking for someone who is listening. Be ready. When God opens a door of opportunity, be ready to walk through it. Be involved. Find out how you can serve the Lord through your church. Before you can lead, you need to serve. Serve Christ through commitment to your local church. Finally, be in prayer. When Billy Graham was asked about the success of his crusades, he stated that success was due to three things: prayer, prayer, and prayer. Pray that God will use you to make an impact!

ENGAGING ENDEAVORS

What is the biggest revelation you have had during this thirty-day journey?

How has God changed your vision for your mission on earth?

DAILY TAKEAWAY

FROM TODAY'S DEVO -

WRITE SOMETHING DOWN.

_____

_____

_____

_____

_____

_____

PRAY SOMETHING THROUGH.

_____

_____

_____

_____

_____

_____

PASS SOMETHING ALONG.

_____

_____

_____

_____

_____

_____

Closing Challenge

For thirty days, we have walked through the challenges, opportunities and concerns of emerging from the shadows and engaging our world. It is now up to you. I am reminded of a story of a young boy who had a dog. A man asked the boy what type of dog he had. The boy said, "It is a police dog." The man replied, "It does not look like a police dog." To which the boy said, "You are right, he is undercover."

Most of us are trying to live our lives for Jesus "undercover" from the world, but it is time for us to engage our world. Let's start today by engaging just one person with the Gospel of Jesus not worried about anything we can gain or achieve, but by living our lives for His glory.

As this book ends, your journey is just beginning. Life is much more than can be captured on a few pages. You must seek the Lord daily and lean on His Word for strength. We are anxious to see what the Lord is going to do in your life and want to hear about it. If not us, your pastor, youth pastor, and church want to know what God is doing in your life. The real hero in my opinion is not a concert artist or itinerant speaker, but the man or woman God has placed in your life for this journey. So, stay focused on Jesus and faithful to His church and we will see a change take place!

appendix:

DAILY READING PLAN

Below you will find a list of scriptures that correspond to each day of the journey you just completed. For the next 30 days, will you commit to going back through these scriptures and seeing if there are anymore God might have in there for you? Get a clean notebook and start this extension of your journey by taking each day and writing down new insights that God will show you through the second round of these scriptures.

PART I: EMERGE FROM

Day 1
2 Samuel 22:29

Day 2
Psalm 139:14
Colossians 1:16
Daniel 1:8
John 3:3
2 Corinthians 5:17
1 John 3:1
Ephesians 1:6
John 1:12
John 15:14
Romans 8:17
1 Corinthians 6:19
1 Corinthians 12:27
Colossians 2:10
Romans 8:1
2 Corinthians 5:17
Colossians 3:12
2 Timothy 1:7
2 Corinthians 6:1
Ephesians 2:18
Hebrews 13:5

Day 3
1 Peter 5:5
Proverbs 16:18
1 Peter 5:6

Day 4
Colossians 3:13-14

Day 5
Matthew 10:32, 33

Day 6
Matthew 10:37-38

Day 7
Deuteronomy 31:6
Matthew 14
Colossians 3:23
Psalm 139

Day 8
Proverbs 11:13
James 1:19-20, 26
Matthew 12:34
Ephesians 4:29

Day 9
Psalm 39:1
James 3:7-10
2 Corinthians 5:17
Colossians 4:6

Day 10
Proverbs 12:19
Proverbs 12:22
Proverbs 6:16-19

Day 11
Job 31:1
Genesis 2:25
Ephesians 4:19
1 Peter 1:18-19
1 John 1:9

Day 12
Ecclesiastes 2:1
John 12:24
1 Corinthians 15:31

Day 13
Romans 12:2
2 Corinthians 4:4

Day 14
Psalm 46:10
John 10:27
John 18:37
Matthew 13:10-17

Day 15
John 20:27
Luke 7:19
Luke 7: 28

PART II: ENGAGE

Day 16
John 5:24
John 3:7
1 John 1:9
Romans 8:38-39

Day 17
Colossians 3:16

Day 18
Matthew 6:6
2 Corinthians 5:20
Galatians 1:10

Day 19
John 1:3-5

Day 20
Psalm 68:5

Day 21
1 John 4:20
Hebrews 13:1
Proverbs 27:17

Day 22
Romans 15:13
2 Corinthians 4:4
Mark 2:1-12

Day 23
1 Thessalonians 5:17
2 Chronicles 7:14
Jeremiah 33:3

Day 24
2 Corinthians 5:20

Day 25
Psalm 86:11
Isaiah 40:8
Psalm 86:11

Day 26
John 10:30
John 14:6
Jeremiah 29:13
Matthew 7:13-14
John 14:6

Day 27
Deuteronomy 6:6
Daniel 2:31-35
Acts 4:11
Ephesians 2:20
Daniel 2:44
Revelation 11:15
Proverbs 22:28

Day 28
Matthew 24:36, 40, 42
James 4:14
Genesis 3:19
Hebrews 9:27
1 Thessalonians 4:13-14
James 4:13-17

Day 29
James 2:26

Day 30
Matthew 28:19
Acts 1:8

Biographies:

Scott Dawson has a passion to share Christ with this generation. He is the founder and president of Scott Dawson Evangelistic Association that provides a platform to share Christ. Traveling extensively, Scott has shared the message of the Gospel to millions of people through live events and radio. In addition to speaking, he also conducts one of the fastest growing conferences in America called Strength To Stand Student Conference. Scott resides in Birmingham, Alabama with his wife, Tarra and their two children, Hunter and Hope.

As a student pastor, student evangelist and now a senior pastor, God has used Joey Hill all over the country to help students, parents and others shed defeated lives for the glory of God through conferences, camps, revivals and missions. Joey serves in the Conference Department at Scott Dawson Evangelistic Association developing relationships and mentoring student pastors. He, his wife Brownie, and children, Hope, Ivey, Maxon and Tyson live in Warrior, Alabama where Joey serves as Senior Pastor of High Point Community Church.

Despite the tornado of unsettled dust swirling around him, hip-hop veteran KJ-52 refused to play it safe, zigged while so many others zagged, and managed to create what's easily the most mind-bendingly ambitious project of his career, Five-Two Television. Eschewing convention and the party-line siren call of "less is more," KJ-52 instead dives headlong into a new renaissance that at-once captures the dizzying array of galaxies in our media-drenched universe yet ultimately points to the One who holds time, space, the planet and our very lives together.

Scott Lenning worked for the Billy Graham Evangelistic Association for 19 years preparing communities and serving as a Crusade Director for Billy Graham Crusades. He currently serves as the Executive Director for the Scott Dawson Evangelistic Association. Scott also served as the co-director of Mission Africa which was conducted in fellowship with Cape Town 2010: the Third Lausanne Congress on World Evangelization.

A WORD ABOUT THE AUTHORSHIP
This book was co-written by Scott Dawson, Joey Hill and Scott Lenning with special contributor, Jonah Sorrentino - stage name KJ-52 (Emerge Days 4, 5, 6 and Engage Day 4).